Web Scraping with PHP

2nd Edition

by Matthew Turland

Web Scraping with PHP

php[architect] edition published: August 2019

Print ISBN:	978-1-940111-67-4
PDF ISBN:	978-1-940111-68-1
ePub ISBN:	978-1-940111-60-8
Mobi ISBN	978-1-940111-70-4

Produced & Printed in the United States

Disclaimer

Written by
Matthew Turland

Managing Editor
Oscar Merida

Editor
Kara Ferguson

Published by
musketeers.me, LLC.
4627 University Dr
Fairfax, VA 22030 USA

240-348-5PHP (240-348-5747)
info@phparch.com
www.phparch.com

Table of Contents

Foreword

"Web scraping is the future of the Web."

At least, that's what I wrote ten years ago in the foreword to the first edition of the book you hold in your hands. In the intervening decade, much has changed. If we thought *Web 2.0* had ushered in a glorious new era of APIs, then the period that followed—be it *Web 3.0* or whatever we choose to call it—firmly cemented them as a staple of web development. A swell of new technologies, tools, and trends washed over the industry, bringing in a high tide of API proliferation and a greater need than ever to speak the language of HTTP.

Yet, the promise of the Web is still a long way off. We now find ourselves at an awkward crossroads of the Web that was and the Web that will be, and we hold within ourselves the power to decide its fate. The behemoth companies that grew out of the *Web 2.0* revolution have built up walled gardens, making some of us complacent and others jaded. The Web we once used for sharing and furthering culture is now used for spreading hate and vitriol. In response, Yancey Strickler writes, "we're retreating to our dark forests of the internet, and away from the mainstream"[1].

Retreating isn't a bad thing. It can be good for mental health. Sometimes, it's necessary to turn off, tune out, and take a break. Unfortunately, retreating also reduces our influence at a time when it really matters.

When the Web began, its purpose was to share data. The educational and research communities used the Web to display data and link it through hyperlinks to other data. Since JSON and, much less, web APIs did not exist in the early days. It became common practice to write scripts to fetch data from other websites, parse the HTML received, process the data in some way, and then display it on one's website.

One of my earliest experiences with web scraping was in 1998, when I wanted to display up-to-date news headlines on a website. At the time, there was a news website providing HTML snippets of headlines for its customers to embed on their websites. I, however, was not a customer, but I figured out a way to grab the raw HTML, parse it, and display it on my website. As unethical as this may have been, I was participating in what I would later find out is called "web scraping."

And this was the essence of the young Web. Data is valuable. Data is *empowering*. Data wants to be free. You can't lock it up. It will escape. In a 2009 TED Talk, Tim Berners-Lee proclaimed, "We want

---

[1] Yancey Strickler, "The Dark Forest Theory of the Internet," *Medium*, May 20, 2019, *https://phpa.me/onezero-dark-forest-theory*.

the data. We want unadulterated data. We have to ask for raw data now"[2]. Web scraping unlocks the data. It gets it out of the silos and liberates it. APIs are not the only means to transport data on the Web—they often serve as the largest gatekeepers, blocking access to all manner of information. Web pages are the original web APIs! The data within them is meant to be used, and it should be linked to other data on other websites.

Now, more than ever, we must return to the original ideals of the Web. Yes, the Web may be used for business and commerce, but it is also the greatest disseminator of culture history has ever known. If we retreat into our dark forests, we condemn the Web to an information Dark Age. Business will continue to innovate, and technology will continue to evolve, but without our influence, culture and information will grow stale and stagnant, further enabling the Web as "an engine of inequity and division"[3].

I am heartened by initiatives such as the IndieWeb movement[4], Tim Berners-Lee's Solid project[5], recommendations produced by the W3C Social Web Working Group, and other efforts to blur and destroy the walls separating our online spaces. Through their efforts to federate our online experiences, these projects aim to return control of personal and private data to individuals and provide the means to open up public data to the masses. However, this is not enough. All of us must commit to use our influence to create a better Web.

My challenge to you is this: liberate your data. Do not retreat into the dark forests. Build a website for yourself, and don't worry if it's not beautiful or your writing contains typos and grammatical errors—it is your place on the Web to share with others. If you have data to share, especially if you are a company, make it available for others to use—even better if you use microformats or some other standard to describe your data, making it easier for others to parse. Link your data to other data. Don't lock it up behind an API gate. Scrape websites. Don't get data just from APIs. Consume the HTML of a web page and parse it.

Over the last ten years, web scraping hasn't been utilized enough, and yet, I still believe it holds the key to the future of the Web. Within these pages, you'll learn all the tools and tricks you need to scrape websites effectively. What you do with the data is yours to decide, but please, whatever you do, don't lock it away. Make it available for others to scrape again and remix for their uses.

Web scraping is the future of the Web. Remixing is the future of our culture.

Ben Ramsey

Nashville, Tennessee

June 28, 2019

---

[2]   Tim Berners-Lee, "The Next Web," TED, February 2009,
      https://www.ted.com/talks/tim_berners_lee_on_the_next_web.
[3]   Tim Berners-Lee, "One Small Step for the Web," Medium, September 29, 2018,
      https://phpa.me/berners-lee-one-small-step.
[4]   IndieWeb, https://indieweb.org.
[5]   Solid, https://solid.inrupt.com.

Acknowledgements

This section probably isn't why you purchased this book, but I encourage you to read on anyway. One of the things I learned during my time in college is, even if I don't retain all that is taught to me, having even a vague awareness of that knowledge serves to broaden and improve my perspective. I believe the same is true of knowing more about the author when reading a book they've written, in particular the people who contributed to that person's life and perseverance through the completion of their work. The people described here are good people and they deserve to be remembered.

Brandi

It takes a lot for a spouse to support and encourage your work on a project as demanding as writing a book, especially when that project takes from their time with you and your time with other hobbies and pursuits. This second edition was quite a long time in the making. You would not be reading it now were it not for them actively pushing me to complete it.

php[architect]

The amount of change that has happened within the PHP community since the first edition caused the book to show its age. Thank you for the opportunity to freshen up my first work and facilitating the existence and polish of this book.

Ben Ramsey

Ben is a man for whom I have immense respect. He is willing to assert his opinions, including the importance of developing and adhering to web standards. Our discussions on topics from the HTTP protocol to interpretation of Roy Fielding's dissertation on REST have engaged and inspired me. As the completion of this book's first edition neared, I began to consider how much it would merit from a foreword by someone with his expertise when it was published. When I approached him about it and asked if he would do the honors, he happily accepted. Later, as I considered what content from the original edition to include in this one, I found his foreword still held relevance and decided to ask him to update it for this edition.

Friends

The term "friend" is not one I use lightly. It has long been a belief of mine that family is not something held within a bloodline, but in how people treat one another, and I hold friends in the same regard. There is a special group of people within the PHP community to whom I apply this term. They are too many to name, but each has at one point or another offered critique, suggestion, or moral support whenever I needed it. I think each will know who they are. However small they might consider what they gave, I hope they know its importance and my gratitude for it.

You

While it can take a while longer to write one, time spent reading a book is also a personal investment. This book has made its way through a long journey of development to your hands. You are its audience. I appreciate the time you're taking to read this book and hope it proves to be time well spent. Regardless of what your opinion of it might be once you've read it, I encourage you to write a review, discuss it on your preferred social networking site, or e-mail me at _me@matthewturland.com_ and let me know what your thoughts are.

Chapter

1

Introduction

This chapter gives you an idea of what this book is about and defines who should find it useful. It provides some background on the material covered and addresses some common and pertinent concerns. If you have a good high-level idea of what web scraping is and would like to jump straight into the more technical content in this book, you can skip on ahead to the *next chapter*.

Intended Audience

This book targets developers of an intermediate or advanced level who already have a fair amount of comfort programming with PHP. You should be aware of object-oriented programming principles such as inheritance, abstraction, and encapsulation as well as how these principles relate to the PHP object model. Code examples in the book assume use of PHP 7 but should work in PHP 5 as well unless otherwise noted. The book details general concepts and uses PHP as a qualified means to an end of illustrating these concepts with practical examples. Knowledge of the HTTP protocol, XML concepts, related PHP extensions, and some familiarity with JavaScript should also prove helpful.

How to Read This Book

If you come across an unfamiliar PHP function, point your preferred web browser at `http://php.net/functionname` where `functionname` is the name of the function in question. This URL generally takes you to either the function's entry in the manual or the landing page for the manual section which contains that function entry.

You are highly recommended to read *Chapter 2*, as it provides context to later chapters related to HTTP clients. Beyond that, you can read the chapters independently, but they do interrelate in such a way that reading the book from cover to cover may be useful to form a thorough understanding of the material.

Web Scraping Defined

Web scraping is a process involving the retrieval of a semi-structured document from the internet and analysis of that document to extract specific data from it for use in another context. Generally, this is a web page in a markup language such as HTML or XHTML. Web scraping is commonly (though not entirely accurately) also known as screen scraping. It does not technically fall within the field of data mining because the latter implies an attempt to discern semantic patterns or trends in large data sets that are already obtained. Web scraping applications (also called intelligent, automated, or autonomous agents) focus on obtaining the data itself through retrieval and extraction and can involve data sets of varied sizes.

You might be saying to yourself web scraping sounds a lot like acting as a client for a web service. The difference is in the intended audience of the document and, by proxy, the document's format and structure. Web services must return data of a consistently formatted structure parsable by machines, ranging from JSON to rigidly defined XML schemas.

By contrast, web browsers are generally a lot more forgiving about handling the visual rendering of a document when its markup is not valid. People authored the first web pages manually, so browsers had to be lenient in how they interpreted HTML for rendering. Of course, this led to different browsers interpreting the same HTML markup in slightly different ways. Nowadays, with more sophisticated tools, this problem may not be as common. With so much HTML markup available, though, assuming it will always be well-structured is infeasible.

Web browsers are also intended for human use, and the methods in which they consume information do not always fall parallel to the way machines would consume it when using a web service. This can make the development of web scraping applications challenging. Like the obligation of a web service to generate a valid response, a web browser has certain responsibilities. These include respecting server requests not to index individual pages and keeping the number of requests sent to servers within a reasonable amount.

In short, web scraping is the subset of a web browser's functionality necessary to retrieve and render data in a manner conducive to the use of that data.

Applications of Web Scraping

Though it's becoming more common for web sites to expose their data using web services, the absence of a data source tailored to machines that offers all the data of a corresponding web site is still a common situation. In these instances, the web site itself must effectively become your data source, and you can use web scraping to automate the consumption of the data it makes available. Web services are also used to transfer information into external data systems. In their absence, you can use web scraping to integrate with web-based interfaces for their users.

Another more prevalent application of web scraping is the development of automated agents known as crawlers, which seek out resources for storage and analysis that comprise the search results they deliver to you. In the earliest days of the internet, humans manually sought out data of this type and organized it into sites like Yahoo! Directory and DMOZ. This curation was a slow and tedious process that limited the speed at which a site could expand its content offerings. Web scraping provided an alternative to allow computers to do the grunt work of finding new pages and extracting their content.

Lastly, web scraping is one way—not the sole way or necessarily the recommended way, but certainly a way—to write integration and system tests for web applications. Using its abilities to act as a client in extracting and transmitting data, a web scraping application can simulate the browser activity of a human user. This mimicry can help to ensure web application output complies with its requirements.

Appropriate Use of Web Scraping

Some data providers may offer a web site with no API, while others may offer APIs that do not offer the desired data in a conducive format or at all. Some web services may involve an extensive authentication process or be unavailable for public consumption. Lack of availability or reliability of web service endpoints compared to web sites may also make them infeasible to use. In situations like these, web scraping becomes a desirable alternative.

It's common practice to avoid making changes that break backward-compatibility with existing applications using web service APIs, or to version them to allow application vendors time to transition to new revisions. As such, web services are less prone to change than the markup structure of pages on a web site, and changes to the former generally come with more advance warning. Sites that change frequently can drastically affect the stability of web scraping applications.

In summary, use web scraping as a last resort when there are no other options for acquiring the needed data.

Legality of Web Scraping

The answer to this question is a bit extensive and veers off into "legal land." As such, it's included in *Appendix A* to avoid detracting from the primary purpose of the book.

Topics Covered

- Chapter 1, the one you're reading now, provides a brief introduction to web scraping, answers common questions, and leads into the meat of the book.
- Chapter 2 deals with relevant details of the HTTP protocol, as document retrieval involves HTTP clients. This includes structure of requests and responses, as well as headers used for features such as cookies, HTTP authentication, redirection, and more.
- Chapters 3–7 cover specific PHP HTTP client libraries and their features, usage, and advantages and disadvantages of each.
- Chapter 8 goes into developing a custom client library and common concerns when using any library including prevention of throttling, access randomization, agent scheduling, and side effects of client-side scripts.
- Chapter 9 details the use of the tidy extension for correcting issues with retrieved markup before using other extensions to analyze it.
- Chapters 10–12 review XML extensions for PHP, compare and contrast the two classes of XML parsers, and provide a brief introduction to XPath.
- Chapter 13 is a study of CSS selectors, comparisons between them and XPath expressions, and information on available libraries for using them to query markup documents.
- Chapter 14 reviews components from the Symfony project useful for working with HTML documents.
- Chapter 15 explores regular expressions using the PCRE extension, which can be useful in extracting data and then validating the scraped data to ensure the stability of the web scraping application.
- Chapter 16 reviews typical practical applications as well as general high-level strategies and best practices for designing and developing your web scraping applications.

Chapter

2

HTTP

The first task a web scraping application must be capable of performing is the retrieval of documents containing the information to extract. If you have used a web browser without becoming aware of all it does "under the hood" to render a page for your viewing pleasure, this may sound trivial to you. The complexity of a web scraping application is generally proportional to the complexity of the application it targets for retrieving and extracting data.

For targets consisting of more than one page or requiring retention of session or authentication information, some level of reverse-engineering is often required to develop a corresponding web scraping application. Like a complex mathematics problem with a simple answer, the development of web scraping applications can sometimes involve more analysis of the target than work to write a script capable of retrieving and extracting data from it.

This sort of reconnaissance requires a decent working knowledge of the **HyperText Transfer Protocol** or **HTTP**, the protocol that powers the internet. This chapter focuses on familiarization with that protocol. The end goal is becoming capable of performing the necessary research to learn how a target application works such that you are capable of writing an application to extract the data you want.

Requests

The HTTP protocol gives two parties a common method of communication: **web clients** and **web servers**. Clients are programs or scripts which send requests to servers. Examples of clients include web browsers, such as Mozilla Firefox and Google Chrome, and crawlers, like those used by Bing and Google to expand their search engine offerings. Servers are programs that run indefinitely and do nothing but receive and send responses to client requests. Popular examples include the Apache HTTP Server and NGINX.

You must be familiar with the anatomy and nuances of HTTP requests and responses for two reasons. First, you must be able to configure and use your preferred client to view requests and responses that pass between it and the server hosting the target application as you access it. This is essential to developing your web scraping application without expending an excessive amount of time and energy on your part.

Second, you must be able to use most of the features offered by a PHP HTTP client library. Ideally, you would know HTTP and PHP well enough to build your client library or fix issues with an existing one if necessary. In principle, though, you should resort to finding and using an adequate existing library first and constructing a reusable one as a last resort. We examine some of these libraries in the next chapters.

Supplemental References

This book covers HTTP as it relates to web scraping, but you should not in any respect consider it a comprehensive guide on the subject. Here are some recommended references to supplement the material covered in this book.

- RFC 6265 HTTP State Management Mechanism, *https://tools.ietf.org/html/rfc6265*
- RFC 7230 Hypertext Transfer Protocol (HTTP/1.1): Message Syntax and Routing, *https://tools.ietf.org/html/rfc7230*
- RFC 7231 Cryptographic Algorithm Implementation Requirements and Usage Guidance, *https://tools.ietf.org/html/rfc7321*
- RFC 7232 Hypertext Transfer Protocol (HTTP/1.1): Conditional Requests, *https://tools.ietf.org/html/rfc7232*
- RFC 7233 Hypertext Transfer Protocol (HTTP/1.1): Range Requests, *https://tools.ietf.org/html/rfc7233*
- RFC 7234 Hypertext Transfer Protocol (HTTP/1.1): Caching *https://tools.ietf.org/html/rfc7234*
- RFC 7235 Hypertext Transfer Protocol (HTTP/1.1): Authentication, *https://tools.ietf.org/html/rfc7235*
- RFC 6874 Representing IPv6 Zone Identifiers in Address Literals and Uniform Resource Identifiers, *https://tools.ietf.org/html/rfc6874*
- RFC 7320 URI Design and Ownership, *https://tools.ietf.org/html/rfc7320*

- *Learning HTTP/2: A Practical Guide for Beginners* by Stephen Ludin and Javier Garza (ISBN 1491962445)
- *HTTP: The Definitive Guide* by David Gourley and Brian Totty (ISBN 1565925092)
- *HTTP Pocket Reference: HyperText Transfer Protocol* by Clinton Wong (ISBN 1565928628)
- *HTTP Developer's Handbook* by Chris Shiflett (ISBN 0672324547)
- Ben Ramsey's blog series on *HTTP Status Codes, http://benramsey.com/http-status-codes*

GET Requests

Let's start with a simple HTTP request, one to retrieve the main landing page of Wikipedia in English.

```
GET /wiki/Main_Page HTTP/1.1
Host: en.wikipedia.org
```

The individual components of this request are as follows.

- GET is the **method** or **operation**. Think of it as a verb in a sentence, an action you want to perform on something. Other examples of methods include POST and HEAD. This chapter covers these in more detail later.
- /wiki/Main_Page is the **Uniform Resource Identifier** or **URI**. It provides a unique point of reference for the **resource**, the object or target of the operation.
- HTTP/1.1 specifies the HTTP **protocol version** in use by the client, detailed further later in this chapter.
- The method, URL, and HTTP version collectively make up the **request line**, which ends with a (carriage return-line feed) sequence, which corresponds to ASCII characters 13 and 10 or Unicode characters U+000D and U+000A respectively. (See RFC 7230 Section 1.2 for more information.)
- A single **header** Host and its associated value en.wikipedia.org follow the request line. More header-value pairs may follow.
- Based on the resource, the value of the Host header, and the protocol in use (HTTP, as opposed to HTTPS or HTTP over SSL), http://en.wikipedia.org/wiki/Main_Page is the resulting full URL of the requested resource.

URI Versus URL

URI is sometimes used interchangeably with URL, which frequently leads to confusion about the exact nature of either. A URI uniquely identifies a resource, indicates how to locate a resource, or both. URL is the subset of URI that does both (as opposed to either) and is what makes them usable by humans. After all, what's the use of being able to identify a resource if you can't access it! See sections 1.1.3 and 1.2.2 of RFC 3986 for more information.

GET is by far the most commonly used operation in the HTTP protocol. According to the HTTP specification, the intent of GET is to request a representation of a resource, essentially to "read" it as you would a file on a file system. Common examples of formats for such representations include HTML, JSON, and XML-based formats such as XHTML, RSS, and Atom.

In principle, GET should strictly be a read operation and should not change any existing data exposed by the application. For this reason, it's called a **safe operation**. It's worth noting that may encounter situations where target applications use GET operations incorrectly to change data. This indicates poor application design and you should doing so when developing your applications.

Anatomy of a URL

Let's review the components of a URL. This will be useful in later chapters.

```
http://user:pass@www.example.com:8080/path/to/file.ext?query=&var=value#anchor
```

- http is the protocol used to interact with the resource. Another example is https, which is http used on an encrypted connection using an SSL certificate.
- user:pass@ is an optional component that informs the client that the resource requires Basic HTTP authentication to access and that it should use user and pass for the username and password respectively when authenticating. The end of this chapter covers HTTP authentication in more detail.
- example.com is the hostname identifying the web server with which the client communicates.
- :8080 is another optional segment used to instruct the client that 8080 is the port on which the web server listens for incoming requests. In the absence of this segment, most clients use the standard HTTP port 80.
- /path/to/file.ext specifies the resource to access.
- query=&var=value is the query string, which the next section covers in more depth.
- #anchor is the fragment, which points to a specific location within or state of the current resource.

PHP can parse these with parse_url()[1] and parse_str()[2].

```
$url = 'http://user:pass@www.example.com:8080/path/to/file.ext?query=&var=value#anchor';
$parsed_url = parse_url($url);

var_export($parsed_url);
```

---

[1]   parse_url(): *http://php.net/function.parse-url*
[2]   parse_str(): *http://php.net/function.parse-str*

Output:

```
array (
  'scheme' => 'http',
  'host' => 'www.example.com',
  'port' => 8080,
  'user' => 'user',
  'pass' => 'pass',
  'path' => '/path/to/file.ext',
  'query' => 'query=&var=value',
  'fragment' => 'anchor',
)
```

We can use parts parsed from the URL:

```
$query = $parsed_url['query'];
parse_str($query, $parsed_query);
var_export($parsed_query);
```

Output:

```
array (
  'query' => '',
  'var' => 'value',
)
```

Query Strings

Another provision of URLs is a mechanism called the **query string** which passes **request parameters** to web applications. Below is a GET request which includes a query string and accesses a form to edit a page on Wikipedia.

```
GET /w/index.php?title=Query_string&action=edit
Host: en.wikipedia.org
```

There URL has some notable traits.

- A question mark (?) denotes the end of the resource path and the beginning of the query string.
- Key-value pairs make up the query string and an ampersand (&) separates each pair.
- An equal sign (=) separates keys and values.

Note that it's possible to encounter encoded ampersands in cases where markup contains embedded URLs, such as in HTML documents containing hyperlinks. Use html_entity_decode()[3] to decode the ampersands in such cases.

---

[3]   html_entity_decode(): *http://php.net/function.html-entity-decode*

Query strings are not specific to GET operations; other operations use them as well. Speaking of which, let's move on.

> ### Query String Limits
>
> *Though RFC 7230 imposes none, most mainstream browsers impose a limit on the character length of a query string. There's no standardized value for this, but querying a search engine should turn up your preferred browser's limit. It's rare for this to become an issue during development, but it's a circumstance worth knowing.*

POST Requests

The next most common HTTP operation after GET is POST, which submits data to a specified resource. When using a web browser as a client, this is most often done via an HTML form.

POST adds to or alters data exposed by the application, a potential result of which is the creation of a new resource, or changes to an existing resource. As such, POST requests are not **idempotent**, meaning you cannot repeat them with the expectation that they will produce the same result each time.

> *At the core, idempotent requests are operations which always return the same response. GET and PUT requests are idempotent. The former always returns the same response while the latter updates the same resource without a change in outcomes. POST and DELETE are not idempotent since they can create or destroy a resource.*

One major difference between a GET request and a POST request is the latter includes a **body** following the request headers to contain the data to submit.

```
POST /w/index.php?title=Wikipedia:Sandbox&action=submit HTTP/1.1
Host: en.wikipedia.org
Content-Type: application/x-www-form-urlencoded

wpAntispam=&wpSection=&wpStarttime=20080719022313&wpEdittime=20080719022100
&&wpScrolltop=&wpTextbox1=%7B%7BPlease+leave+this+line+alone+%28sandbox+
heading%29%7D%7D+%3C%21--+Hello%21+Feel+free+to+try+your+formatting+and+
editing+skills+below+this+line.+As+this+page+is+for+editing+experiments%2C+
this+page+will+automatically+be+cleaned+every+12+hours.+--%3E+&wpSummary=
&wpAutoSummary=d41d8cd98f00b204e9800998ecf8427e&wpSave=Save+page&wpPreview=
Show+preview&wpDiff=Show+changes&wpEditToken=%5C%2B
```

A single blank line separates the headers from the body. This particular body should look familiar, as its format is identical to the query string with the exception that lacks the leading question mark. While request bodies can take on other formats, this is the one most commonly used. Another common format is JSON, which is typically returned by web services and used as a general format for data exchange.

> **URL Encoding**
>
> *One trait of query strings is that percent-encoding or, as it's more commonly known,* **URL encoding**. *The PHP functions* urlencode()[4] *and* urldecode()[5] *are a convenient way to handle string values encoded in this manner. Encoded characters include those that can have special significance in URLs such as spaces, colons, forward slashes, ampersands, question marks, number signs/ hash marks, percent signs, etc. Most HTTP client libraries handle encoding request parameters for you. Though it's called URL encoding, the technical details for it are more often associated with the URI as shown in section 2.1 of RFC 3986.*

HEAD Requests

Though not common when accessing target web applications, HEAD requests are useful in web scraping applications in several ways. They function in the same way as a GET request with one exception: when the server delivers its response, it will not deliver the resource representation in the response body. The reason this is useful is it allows a client to get at the data present in the response headers without having to download the entire response, which is liable to be significantly larger. Such data can include if the resource is still available for access and, if so, when it was last modified.

```
HEAD /wiki/Main_Page HTTP/1.1
Host: en.wikipedia.org
```

Speaking of responses, now would be a good time to investigate those in more detail.

Responses

Aside from the first response line, called the **status line**, responses have a format much like requests. While requests and responses use different headers, the format of those headers is the same. A blank line separates the headers and the body in both requests and responses. The body may or may not be present in requests and responses; this generally depends on what the request operation is. The following is an example response.

---

[4]   urlencode(): *http://php.net/urlencode*
[5]   urldecode(): *http://php.net/urldecode*

```
HTTP/1.0 200 OK
Date: Mon, 21 Jul 2008 02:32:52 GMT
Server: Apache
X-Powered-By: PHP/5.2.5
Cache-Control: private, s-maxage=0, max-age=0, must-revalidate
Content-Language: en
Last-Modified: Mon, 21 Jul 2008 02:06:27 GMT
Content-Length: 53631
Content-Type: text/html; charset=utf-8
Connection: close

[body...]
```

Aside from headers, the main difference in content between requests and responses is in the contents of the request line versus the status line.

- 1.0 is the earliest HTTP protocol version under which which the client can interpret the response.
- 200 is a response **status code** and OK is its corresponding human-readable description. It indicates the result of the server attempting to process the request, in this case that the request was successful.

Status codes have five classes distinguished by the first digit of the code. Below is a summary of each class. See section 6 of RFC 7231[6] for further descriptions of circumstances under which you may receive specific status codes.

Status Code	Description
1xx Informational	Request received, continuing process.
2xx Success	Request received, understood, and accepted.
3xx Redirection	Client must take further action to complete the request.
4xx Client Error	Server could not fulfill the request because of a client issue.
5xx Server Error	Request was valid but the server failed to process it.

Moving right along, let us examine headers in more depth.

Headers

An all-purpose method of communicating a variety of information related to requests and responses, the client and server use headers to maintain state using cookies and verify identity using HTTP authentication. This section deals with those that are applicable to web scraping applications. For more information, see sections 5 and 7 of RFC 7231.

---

[6]   RFC 7231: *https://www.ietf.org/rfc/rfc7231.txt*

Case Sensitivity

Header names are case-insensitive per RFC 7230 Section 3.2. The same applies to most header values, but there are some exceptions to this such as date values (see RFC 7231 Section 7.1.1.2), and media type parameter values (see RFC 6838 Section 4.3). In general, this applies mainly when accessing header values or dealing with client issues related to parsing headers.

Cookies

HTTP is a stateless protocol. That is, once a server returns the response for a request, it effectively "forgets" about the request. It may log information about the request and the response it delivered, but it does not maintain any state for the same client between requests. In essence, this means the server does not keep any information from a client between HTTP requests.

Cookies are a method of circumventing statelessness by using headers. Here is how they work.

1. The client issues a request.
2. In its response, the server includes a Set-Cookie header. The header value contains name-value pairs, each with optional associated attribute-value pairs.
3. In later requests, the client includes a Cookie header containing the data it received in the Set-Cookie response header.

Cookies are frequently used to restrict access to certain content, most often by requiring some form of identity authentication before the target application sets a required cookie. Most client libraries can handle parsing and resending cookie data as appropriate, though some require explicit instruction before they will do so. For more information on cookies, see RFC 2965[7].

The client uses one cookie attribute, expires, to know when it should dispose of the cookie and not persist its data in later requests. This attribute is optional, and its presence or lack thereof is the defining factor in whether or not the cookie is what's called a **session cookie**. If a cookie does not have an expires value, it persists for the duration of the client session. For most web browsers, this session generally concludes when the user closes all instances of the browser application.

Manipulating Cookie Values

Take extreme care when doing anything with Set-Cookie header values beyond including them as Cookie header values in later requests. Web applications often assume clients behave this way. As such, they may contain little or no logic for validating cookie data, so manipulating it on the client side may lead to unpredictable or unexpected results.

---

[7]   RFC 2965: *https://www.ietf.org/rfc/rfc2965.txt*

Redirection

The server uses the Location header to redirect the client to a URI. In this scenario, the response often includes a 3xx class status code (such as 302 Found), but may also include a 201 code to signify the creation of a new resource. See subsection 7.1.2 of RFC 7231 for more information.

A malfunctioning application may start an infinite series of redirects between the server and the client. For this reason, client libraries often impose a limit on the number of consecutive redirects it will process before assuming the accessed application is behaving inappropriately and terminating. Libraries generally impose a default limit, but allow you to override it with your own.

Referring URLs

A requested resource may refer to other resources in some way. When this happens, clients traditionally include the URL of the referring resource in the Referer header. The header name is intentionally misspelled. The commonality of that particular misspelling caused it to end up in the official HTTP specification, thereby becoming the standard industry spelling used when referring to that particular header.

The specification of a referrer can occur under different circumstances. A user may click on a hyperlink in a browser, in which case the full URL of the resource containing the hyperlink would be the referrer. When the client requests a resource containing markup with embedded images, requests for those images contain the full URL of the page containing the images as the referrer. A referrer is also specified when redirection occurs, as described in the previous section.

This is relevant because some applications depend on the value of the Referer header by design. This is less than ideal for the simple fact that the responsibility of sending this header value falls to the client, so it can send any arbitrary value. In any case, be aware that some applications may not function as expected if the provided header value is not consistent with what the application sends when it's used in a browser. See subsection 5.5.2 of RFC 7231 for more information.

Persistent Connections

The standard operating procedure for an HTTP request is as follows.

1. A client connects to a server.
2. The client sends a request over the established connection.
3. The server returns a response.
4. The server terminates the connection.

When sending consecutive requests to the same server, the first and fourth steps in that process can cause a significant amount of overhead. HTTP 1.0 established no solution for this; one connection per request was normal behavior. Between the releases of the HTTP 1.0 and 1.1 standards, a convention was informally established which involved the client including a Connection header with a value of Keep-Alive in the request to ask for a persistent connection.

Later, 1.1 changed the default behavior from one connection per request to persistent connections. For a non-persistent connection, the client could include a Connection header with a value of close to instruct the server to close the connection after it sent the response. This difference between 1.0 and 1.1 is an important distinction and should be a point of examination when evaluating both client libraries and servers hosting target applications so that you are aware of their level of support for persistent connections. See subsection 6.3 of RFC 7230 for more information.

An alternative implementation that has gained less support in clients and servers involves the use of a Keep-Alive header. Appendix A.1.2 of RFC 7230 discusses technical issues with this, but you should avoid explicit use of this header; be aware it exists and relates to the matter of persistent connections.

Content Caching

Two methods exist to allow clients to query servers in order to determine if resources have changed since the client last accessed them. Subsections of RFC 7232 detail related headers.

The first method is time-based where the server returns a Last-Modified header (subsection 2.2) in its response and the client can send that value in an If-Modified-Since header (subsection 3.3) in a later request for the same resource.

The other method is hash-based where the server sends a hash value in its response via the ETag header (subsection 2.3) and the client may send that value in an If-None-Match header (subsection 3.2) in a later request for the same resource.

If the resource has not changed in either instance, the server returns a 304 Not Modified response. Aside from checking to ensure a resource is still available (which results in a 404 Not Found response if it's not), this is an appropriate situation in which to use a HEAD request.

You can invert the logic of the first method using an If-Unmodified-Since header (subsection 3.4), in which case the server returns a 412 Precondition Failed response if the resource has in fact changed since the provided access time.

User Agents

Clients are sometimes referred to as *user agents*. This refers to the fact that web browsers are agents acting on behalf of a user to reduce required intervention on the user's part. The User-Agent header enables the client to provide information about itself, such as its name and version number. Crawlers often use it to provide a URL for obtaining more information about the crawler or the email address of the crawler's operator. A simple search engine query should reveal a list of user agent strings for mainstream browsers. See subsection 5.5.3 of RFC 7231 for more information.

Some applications engage in a practice known as **user agent sniffing** or **browser sniffing** in which they vary the responses they deliver based on the user agent string provided by the client. One common modern application of this is to alter the application response to suit a particular class of device, such as a smartphone or a tablet. In some older sites, this practice can extend to disabling a primary site feature, such as an ecommerce checkout page that uses ActiveX (a technology specific to the Windows operating system and Internet Explorer web browser).

One well-known application of this technique is the robots exclusion standard[8], which explicitly instructs crawlers to avoid accessing individual resources or the entire web site. You should account for the guidelines detailed there when developing a web scraping application to prevent it from exhibiting behavior inconsistent with that of a normal user.

In some cases, a client practice called **user agent spoofing** involving the specification of a false user agent string is enough to circumvent user agent sniffing, but not always. An application may have platform-specific requirements that legitimately warrant it denying access to specific user agents. In any case, avoid spoofing the user agent or having a server-side application rely on its value to the fullest extent possible.

Ranges

The `Range` request header allows the client to specify that server should limit the body of its response to one or more specific byte ranges of the full resource representation. Originally intended to allow failed retrieval attempts to resume from their stopping points, this feature can allow you to reduce data transfer between your application and the server, as well as bandwidth consumption and runtime of your web scraping application.

This is applicable in cases where you have a good rough idea of the location of your target data within the document, or if the document is large and you need a small subset of the data it contains. Using it does add one more variable to the possibility of your application breaking if the target site changes and you should bear that in mind when electing to do so.

While the format of the header value ostensibly allows for other range units, HTTP/1.1 solely supports bytes. The client and server may both use the `Accept-Ranges` header to communicate what units they support. The server will include the range (in a slightly different format) of the full response body containing the partial response body using the `Content-Range` header.

When using bytes as a range unit, 0 represents the beginning of the document. Ranges use inclusive bounds. For example, `0-499` specifies the first 500 bytes of a document. To specify from a point to the end of the document, exclude the later bound. `500-` represents the part of a document beginning from the byte 500 going to its end.

If the client specifies a valid range for the requested resource, the server should return a `206 Partial Content` response. Otherwise, it should return a `416 Requested Range Not Satisfiable` response. See subsections 3.1 and 4.2 of RFC 7233 for more information on the `Range` and `Content-Range` headers respectively.

Basic HTTP Authentication

Another less frequently used method of persisting identity between requests is HTTP authentication. Most third-party clients offer some form of native support for it. It's more commonly used for web services than user-facing web applications these days, but it's good to be aware of how to derive

---

[8]   robots exclusion standard: http://www.robotstxt.org

the appropriate header values in cases where you must write it yourself. For more information on HTTP authentication, see RFC 7235[9].

HTTP authentication comes in "flavors," the more popular two being Basic (unencrypted) and Digest (encrypted). Basic is the more common of the two, but the process for both goes like this.

1. A client sends a request without any authentication information.
2. The server sends a response with a 401 Unauthorized status code and a WWW-Authenticate header.
3. The client re-sends the original request, but this time includes an Authorization header and a corresponding value containing authentication credentials.
4. The server either sends a response indicating success or one with a 403 Forbidden status code indicating that authentication failed.

With Basic authentication, the value of the Authorization header is the word Basic followed by a single space and then a Base64-encoded sequence derived from the username-password pair separated by a colon. If, for example, the username is bigbadwolf and the password is letmein then the value of the header would be Basic YmlnYmFkd29sZjpsZXRtZWlu where the Base64-encoded version of the string bigbadwolf:letmein is what follows Basic.

```
$username = 'bigbadwolf';
$password = 'letmein';
$header = 'Basic ' . base64_encode($username . ':' . $password);
```

Note that you can skip steps one and two shown above if the client already has an Authorization header value to include in its request. Some clients also provide support for specifying the username-password pair in the request URL and handle deriving and including the appropriate Authorization request header automatically in that case. See the earlier section of this chapter entitled *Anatomy of a URL* for more information on how to do this.

> **Warning:** *Keep in mind Basic authentication uses Base64 to encode the username and password. You can decode these with the* base64_decode()*[10] function. Since Basic authentication does not include password encryption, you should only use it over an encrypted protocol like HTTPS.*

Digest HTTP Authentication

Digest authentication is a bit more involved. The WWW-Authenticate header returned by the server contains the word Digest followed by a single space and then key-value pairs in the format key="value" separated by commas. Below is an example of this header.

---

[9] RFC 7235: *https://www.rfc-editor.org/rfc/rfc7235.txt*
[10] base64_decode(): *https://php.net/base64_decode*

```
WWW-Authenticate: Digest realm="testrealm@host.com",
                         qop="auth,auth-int",
                         nonce="dcd98b7102dd2f0e8b11d0f600bfb0c093",
                         opaque="5ccc069c403ebaf9f0171e9517f40e41"
```

The client must respond with a specific response value that the server verifies before allowing the client to proceed. To derive that value requires use of the MD5 hash algorithm, which PHP implements in the md5()[11] or hash()[12] functions. Here is the process.

1. Concatenate the appropriate username, the value of the realm key provided by the server, and the appropriate password together separated by colons and take the MD5 hash of that string. We'll call this ha1. It shouldn't change for the rest of the session.

    ```
    $ha1 = md5($username . ':testrealm@host.com:' . $password);
    ```

2. Concatenate the method and URI of the original request separated by a colon and take the MD5 hash of that string. We'll call this ha2. This varies with your method or URI.

    ```
    $ha2 = md5('GET:/wiki/Main_Page');
    ```

3. Initialize a request counter that we'll call nc with a value of 1. Each request increments and transmits the value of this counter to uniquely identify that request. Retransmitting a request counter value used in a previous request results in the server rejecting it. Note that the server expects the client to express this counter value as a hexadecimal number. dechex()[13] is useful for this.

    ```
    $nc = dechex(1);
    ```

4. Using either of the md5() or hash() functions, generate a random hash that we'll call the client nonce or cnonce. random_int()[14] or random_bytes()[15] in PHP 7 or openssl_random_pseudo_bytes()[16] in older PHP versions, used in combination with bin2hex()[17], may be useful for this. You can (and should) regenerate and resend this with each request.

    ```
    $cnonce = bin2hex(openssl_random_pseudo_bytes(64));
    ```

5. Take note of the value of the nonce key provided by the server, also known as the server nonce. We'll refer to this as the nonce. This is randomly generated by the server and expires after a certain period, at which point the server responds with a 401 Unauthorized status code. It modifies the WWW-Authenticate header it returns in two noteworthy ways: 1) it adds the key-value pair stale=TRUE; 2) it changes the nonce value. When this happens, re-derive the response code

---

[11] md5(): *http://php.net/md5*
[12] hash(): *http://php.net/hash*
[13] dechex(): *http://php.net/dechex*
[14] random_int(): *http://php.net/function.random-int*
[15] random_bytes(): *http://php.net/function.random-bytes*
[16] openssl_random_pseudo_bytes(): *http://php.net/function.openssl-random-pseudo-bytes*
[17] bin2hex(): *http://php.net/function.bin2hex*

as shown below with the new nonce value and resubmit the original request (not forgetting to increment the request counter).

6. Concatenate ha1, the server nonce (nonce), the current request counter (nc) value, the client nonce you generated (cnonce), an appropriate value (e.g. "auth") from the comma-separated list contained in the qop (quality of protection) key provided by the server, and ha2 together separated by colons and take the MD5 hash of that string. This is the final response code.

```
$response = implode(':', [
    $ha1, $nonce, dechex($nc), $cnonce, 'auth', $ha2
]);
```

7. Lastly, send everything the server originally sent in the WWW-Authenticate header, plus the response value and its constituents except the password, back to the server in the usual Authorization header.

```
Authorization: Digest username="USERNAME",
                      realm="testrealm@host.com",
                      nonce="dcd98b7102dd2f0e8b11d0f600bfb0c093",
                      uri="/wiki/Main_Page",
                      qop="auth",
                      nc=00000001,
                      cnonce="0a4f113b",
                      response="6629fae49393a05397450978507c4ef1",
                      opaque="5ccc069c403ebaf9f0171e9517f40e41"
```

Some third-party clients support this; some don't. Again, digest authentication is not commonly used, but it's good to be aware of how to derive the appropriate header value in cases where you must write it yourself. For more information on HTTP authentication, see RFC 7235.

Evolution of HTTP

The HTTP protocol was first documented in 1991. Since then, it has evolved to include more features and has remained relevant through events like the Browsers Wars and the advent of AJAX. In recent years, need for more evolution has risen as the needs of internet users and software developers continue to grow and change.

In 2009, Google announced SPDY, an application-layer protocol which modifies HTTP communication to reduce latency. While some mainstream web browsers and servers have adopted this standard, no PHP HTTP client libraries of note support it yet. Libraries implementing the SPDY standard, such as Spdylay, are under consideration for inclusion in libraries such as libcurl, which backs the PHP cURL extension.

First drafts of the HTTP 2.0 standard built on Google's work on SPDY. 2.0 is like 1.1, but changes framing and transport of data between clients and the server. The final 2.0 specification published in May 2015 in RFC 7540[18] did not require TLS or SSL usage, as some proponents wanted, but all major browsers will solely support HTTP/2 over TLS.

In 2018, work began on HTTP/3 based on an RFC for HTTP over Quick, an experimental transport layer network protocol.

In short, do not let your study of this subject matter end with this chapter or even this book. It's a space that is continuing to change with time to make the web better as a whole, and your attention to these developments benefits you applications.

---

[18]   RFC 7540: *https://tools.ietf.org/html/rfc7540*

Chapter

3

HTTP Streams Wrapper

At this point, you should be reasonably well-acquainted with some of the general concepts involved in using an HTTP client. The next chapters review some of the more popular mainstream client libraries, including common use cases and the advantages and disadvantages of each. The client covered in this chapter is the HTTP streams wrapper[1].

PHP 4.3 saw the addition of the Streams extension to the core. According to the related section of the PHP manual, the intention was to provide "a way of generalizing file, network, data compression, and other operations which share a common set of functions and uses." One of the concepts that streams introduced was the **wrapper**. The job of a wrapper is to define how a stream handles communications in a specific protocol or using a specific encoding. One such protocol for which a wrapper is available is HTTP.

The primary advantages of the HTTP streams wrapper are its ease of use and availability. Its API is minimal; it's easy and quick to get something simple working. The HTTP streams wrapper is part

---

[1]   HTTP streams wrapper: *http://php.net/wrappers.http*

of the PHP core; thus, it's available in all PHP installations, as opposed to an optional extension that may not be, and has no other installation requirements.

The disadvantage of the HTTP streams wrapper is its minimal feature set. It gives you the ability to send HTTP requests without having to construct them entirely on your own (by specifying the body and optionally any headers you want to add) and access data in the response. That's about it. The ability to debug requests is one example of a feature it does not include at the time of this writing.

The fact that the wrapper is C code is a bit of a double-edged sword. On the positive side, there is a significant performance difference between C code and PHP code (though it's more noticeable in a high load environment). On the negative side, you have to either know C or depend on the community to deliver patches for any issues which may arise. This also applies to extensions written in C covered in later sections.

Simple Request and Response Handling

Here's a simple example of the HTTP streams wrapper in action.

```
$response = file_get_contents('http://example.com');
print_r($http_response_header);
```

Some notes:

- You must enable the allow_url_fopen PHP configuration setting for this to work, it's enabled in most environments.
- In this example, file_get_contents()[2] makes a GET request for the specified URL http://example.com.
- $response will contain the response body after the call to the file_get_contents() function completes.
- $http_response_header is implicitly populated with the HTTP response status line and headers after the file_get_contents() call because it uses the HTTP streams wrapper *within the current scope*.

While this example does work, it violates a core principle of good coding practices: no unexpected side effects. The origin of $http_response_header is not entirely obvious because PHP populates it implicitly. It's also more restrictive because the variable is unavailable outside the scope containing the call to file_get_contents(). Here's a better way to get access to the same data from the response headers.

```
$handle = fopen('http://example.com', 'r');
$response = stream_get_contents($handle);
$meta = stream_get_meta_data($handle);
print_r($meta['wrapper_data']);
```

---

[2]   file_get_contents(): *http://php.net/file_get_contents*

Let's step through this.

1. `fopen()` opens a connection to the URL `http://example.com`; the resource `$handle` references a stream for that connection.

2. `stream_get_contents()` reads the remaining data on the stream pointed to by the `$handle` resource into `$response`.

3. `stream_get_meta_data()` reads metadata for the stream pointed to by the `$handle` resource into `$meta`.

4. At this point, `$meta['wrapper_data']` contains the same array as `$http_response_header` would within the current scope. You can call `stream_get_metadata()` with `$handle` in any scope in which the latter is available. This makes it more flexible than `$http_response_header`.

Stream Contexts and POST Requests

Another concept introduced by streams is the **context**[3], which is a set of configuration options used in a streams operation. `stream_context_create()` receives an associative array of context options and their corresponding values and returns a context. When using the HTTP streams wrapper, one use of contexts is to make POST requests, as the wrapper uses the GET method by default.

Listing 3.1

```
1. <?php
2. $context = stream_context_create([
3.     'http' => [
4.         'method' => 'POST',
5.         'header' => implode(
6.             "\r\n", [
7.                 'Content-Type: application/x-www-form-urlencoded',
8.                 'Referer: http://example.com'
9.             ]
10.         ),
11.         'content' => http_build_query([
12.             'param1' => 'value1',
13.             'param2' => 'value2'
14.         ]),
15.     ]
16. ]);
17.
18. $response = file_get_contents(
19.     'http://example.com/process', false, $context
20. );
```

---

[3]   **context**: *http://php.net/context.http*

Here is a walk-through of the example in Listing 3.1.

- 'http' is the streams wrapper used.
- 'POST' is the HTTP method of the request.
- The 'header' stream context setting references a string containing HTTP header key-value pairs, in this case for the Content-Type and Referer HTTP headers. The Content-Type header indicates the request body data is URL-encoded. If you need to set more than one custom header, you must separate them with a carriage return-line feed sequence ("\r\n" also known as a CRLF). implode()[4] is useful for this if you store key-value pairs for headers.
- http_build_query()[5] constructs the body of the request. It can also construct query strings of URLs for GET requests. One useful aspect is that it automatically handles encoding key-value pairs and delimiting them with an ampersand.
- http://example.com/process is the URL of the requested resource.
- file_get_contents()[6] executes the request using options from the context $context created using stream_context_create()[7].
- $response receives the body of the response returned by file_get_contents().

Error Handling

Before PHP 5.3.0, an HTTP streams wrapper operation resulting in an HTTP error response (i.e., a 4xx or 5xx status code) emits a PHP-level warning. This warning contains the HTTP version, the status code, and the status code description. The function calls for such operations generally return false as a result, and leave you without a stream resource to check for more information. Listing 3.2 is an example of how to get what data you can.

Listing 3.2

```php
1.  <?php
2.  function error_handler($errno, $errstr, $errfile, $errline, array $errcontext) {
3.      // $errstr will contain something like this:
4.      // fopen(http:_example.com/404): failed to open stream:
5.      // HTTP request failed! HTTP/1.0 404 Not Found
6.      if ($httperr = strstr($errstr, 'HTTP/')) {
7.          // $httperr will contain HTTP/1.0 404 Not Found in the case
8.          // of the above example, do something useful with that here
9.      }
10. }
11.
12. set_error_handler('error_handler', E_WARNING);
13.
```

---

[4]   implode(): *http://php.net/implode*
[5]   http_build_query(): *http://php.net/http_build_query*
[6]   file_get_contents(): *http://php.net/file_get_contents*
[7]   stream_context_create(): *http://php.net/stream_context_create*

```
14. // If the following statement fails, $stream will be assigned
15. // false and error_handler will be called automatically
16. $stream = fopen('http://example.com/404', 'r');
17.
18. // If error_handler() does not terminate the script, control
19. // will be returned here once it completes its execution
20. restore_error_handler();
```

This situation improved somewhat in PHP 5.3 with the addition of the ignore_errors context setting. When you set this setting to true, PHP treats operations resulting in errors the same way as successful operations and emits no warnings. Listing 3.3 is an example of what it might look like.

Listing 3.3

```php
1.  <?php
2.  $context = stream_context_create([
3.                                      'http' => [
4.                                          'ignore_errors' => true
5.                                      ]
6.                                  ]);
7.
8.  $stream = fopen('http://example.com/404', 'r', false, $context);
9.
10. // $stream will be a stream resource at this point regardless of
11. // the outcome of the operation
12. $body = stream_get_contents($stream);
13. $meta = stream_get_meta_data($stream);
14.
15. // $meta['wrapper_data'][0] will equal something like 'HTTP/1.0 404 Not Found'
16. // at this point, with subsequent array elements being other headers
17. $response = explode(' ', $meta['wrapper_data'][0], 3);
18. list($version, $status, $description) = $response;
19.
20. switch (substr($status, 0, 1)) {
21.     case '4':
22.     case '5':
23.         $result = false;
24.         break;
25.
26.     default:
27.         $result = true;
28. }
```

HTTP Authentication

The HTTP stream wrapper has no context options for HTTP authentication credentials, but you can include credentials as part of the requested URL. See the example below.

```
$response = file_get_contents('http://username:password@example.com');
```

Note that credentials are not pre-encoded; the stream wrapper handles encoding transparently when making the request.

Also, this feature supports Basic HTTP authentication, but you must handle Digest authentication manually. As such, if support for Digest authentication is a desirable feature for your project, consider using a different client library, such as one of the others discussed in later chapters of this book.

More Options

Below are other stream context options for the HTTP streams wrapper that may prove useful.

- 'user_agent' allows you to set the user agent string to use in the operation. You can also set it manually by specifying a value for the User-Agent header in the 'header' context option value.
- 'max_redirects' sets the highest number of redirects that the operation processes before assuming the application is misbehaving and terminating the request. This option is unavailable in PHP versions before 5.1.0 and uses a default value of 20.
- 'follow_location' became available in PHP 5.3.4. If you set 'max_redirects' to 1, the operation will not process redirects, but will emit an error. Setting 'follow_location' to 0 suppresses this error.
- 'timeout' sets a limit on the amount of time in seconds a read operation executes before it terminates. It defaults to the value of the default_socket_timeout PHP configuration setting.

All other features utilizing headers are accessible by specifying request headers in the 'header' context option and checking either $http_response_header or the 'wrapper_data' index of the array returned by stream_get_meta_data()[8] for response headers.

---

[8]   stream_get_meta_data(): _http://php.net/stream_get_meta_data_

Chapter

4

cURL Extension

The cURL PHP extension[1], available since PHP 4.0.2, wraps the libcurl library which implements client logic for a variety of internet protocols including HTTP and HTTPS. Its API is small, and much of the code written to use it sets configuration options and their respective values.

cURL assumes fewer default configuration values[2] than the HTTP streams wrapper, like the number of redirects to process. The disadvantage to this is, combined with the rich feature set of the extension, PHP code to use cURL is often more verbose than code using other client libraries.

Like the streams wrapper, the cURL extension is C code and has the same pros and cons in that respect. cURL uses a **session handle** (of the PHP resource data type) with which you associate configuration settings similar to how they are associated with contexts for stream wrappers. Also, like stream contexts, you can reuse cURL session handles to repeat the same operation until pass them to `curl_close()`.

---

[1]   *cURL PHP extension: http://php.net/book.curl*
[2]   *configuration values: http://php.net/function.curl-setopt*

PHP core bundles the cURL extension, but you must either compile it into PHP or install it[3] as a separate extension. Depending on the runtime environment's operating system, this may involve installing a package, such as the php5-curl package in Debian-based Linux distributions.

You have two methods of checking whether your installation of the PHP cURL extension is successful. If you have shell access to the server, you can run php -m and look for an instance of curl in the output. If not, you can consult the output any of the following function calls from within a PHP script.

```
// inspect php output
phpinfo(\INFO_MODULES);
// inspect array of extensions
var_export(get_loaded_extensions());
// test if a curl_* function exists
var_dump(function_exists('curl_version'));
```

Simple Request and Response Handling

This example performs a simple GET request and stores the body of the response in a variable called $response.

```
$ch = curl_init('http://example.com/');
curl_setopt($ch, CURLOPT_RETURNTRANSFER, true);
$response = curl_exec($ch);
$info = curl_getinfo($ch);
curl_close($ch);
```

Let's look at this line by line.

- curl_init()[4] receives 'http://example.com/' as the URL for the request. Note this parameter is optional and you can specify it by calling curl_setopt() with the cURL session handle ($ch in this case), the CURLOPT_URL constant, and the URL string.

- curl_setopt()[5] sets the configuration setting represented by the CURLOPT_RETURNTRANSFER parameter to have a value of true. This setting causes curl_exec() to return the HTTP response body in a string rather than outputting it directly, the latter being the default behavior.

- curl_exec()[6] executes the request and returns the response body.

- curl_getinfo()[7] obtains information about the last transfer. A later section of this chapter details the specifics on that information.

---

[3]   install it: http://php.net/curl.installation
[4]   curl_init(): http://php.net/curl_init
[5]   curl_setopt(): http://php.net/curl_setopt
[6]   curl_exec(): http://php.net/curl_exec
[7]   curl_getinfo(): http://php.net/curl_getinfo

- `curl_close()`[8] closes the cURL session handle, which is no longer reusable after that point.

A useful setting worth mentioning sooner rather than later is `CURLOPT_VERBOSE`, which outputs debugging information when set to `true`. This sends output to either stderr (the default) or a file handle—not a string which is the file path—referenced by `CURLOPT_STDERR`.

Contrasting GET and POST

The cURL extension has other functions, but most HTTP requests made using the cURL extension follows the sequence of operations shown in the above example. Let's compare this with a POST request in Listing 4.1.

Listing 4.1

```php
1. <?php
2. $data = [
3.     'param1' => 'value1',
4.     'param2' => 'value2',
5.     'file1' => '@/path/to/file',
6.     'file2' => '@/path/to/other/file',
7. ];
8.
9. $ch = curl_init();
10. curl_setopt($ch, CURLOPT_URL, 'http://example.com/process');
11. curl_setopt($ch, CURLOPT_POST, true);
12. curl_setopt($ch, CURLOPT_UPLOAD, true);
13. curl_setopt($ch, CURLOPT_POSTFIELDS, $data);
14. curl_setopt($ch, CURLOPT_RETURNTRANSFER, true);
15. $response = curl_exec($ch);
16. curl_close($ch);
```

Here are the differences between this example and the previous one.

- `curl_setopt()` receives the URL this time instead of `curl_init()`. This is important when reusing cURL session handles with different URLs.
- `CURLOPT_POST` receives a value of `true` to change the request method to POST.
- `CURLOPT_UPLOAD` receives a value of `true` to enable inclusion of files to upload.
- `CURLOPT_POSTFIELDS` is an associative array or pre-formatted query string used as the data for the request body. To upload a file, specify a value where the first character is @ and the rest is a filesystem path to that file.

---

[8]   curl_close(): *http://php.net/curl_close*

> ### Array or String?
>
> *In the PHP manual, there is a note on the page for* curl_setopt() *related to values of the* CURL_POSTFIELDS *setting: "If* value *is an array, the* Content-Type *header will be set to* multipart/form-data*."*
>
> *Some requests made by web scraping applications correspond to HTML* <form> *elements within target web applications. Some target web applications, in particular those written using Microsoft's .NET platform, may produce unexpected output (e.g., returning 500-level HTTP responses) if a web scraping application sends a request containing a* Content-Type *header value that is not consistent with the* enctype *attribute value from the corresponding* <form> *element within the target web application.*
>
> *The default value of this attribute is* application/x-www-form-urlencoded, *which is not used when* CURL_POSTFIELDS *receives an array value. To work around this, pass the array you would use to* http_build_query()[9], *then specify its return value (i.e., a query string for the specified array) as the value for* CURL_POSTFIELDS *instead.*

Here are other cURL configuration setting constants related to the request method.

- CURLOPT_HTTPGET: Boolean that, when set to true, explicitly resets the request method to GET if it's changed from the default.
- CURLOPT_NOBODY: Boolean that, when set to true, excludes the body from the response by changing the request method to HEAD.

Setting Options

curl_setopt_array()[10] allows you to pass in an associative array of setting-value pairs to set with a single function call. Using this results in more concise and readable code as well as fewer function calls for better performance.

Listing 4.2

```php
1. <?php
2. $ch = curl_init();
3.
4. curl_setopt_array($ch, [
5.     CURLOPT_URL => 'http://example.com',
6.     CURLOPT_RETURNTRANSFER => true
7. ]);
8.
9. $response = curl_exec($ch);
10. curl_close($ch);
```

---

[9]   http_build_query(): *http://php.net/http_build_query*
[10] curl_setopt_array(): *http://php.net/curl_setopt_array*

Analyzing Results

By default, curl_getinfo()[11] returns an associative array with information about the last request and response. This information is primarily useful for debugging and analyzing performance issues.

If you need a single element from the array returned by curl_getinfo(), you can in some cases specify a constant representing that element as a second argument to curl_getinfo().

```
$info = curl_getinfo($ch);
$url = $info['url'];

// Equivalent:
$url = curl_getinfo($ch, CURLINFO_EFFECTIVE_URL);
```

Here is a table showing keys from the associative array returned by curl_getinfo() that have corresponding constants. Note the availability of some of these values is dependent on PHP version and the version of the libcurl library used to compile the PHP curl extension.

Key	Constant
'certinfo'	CURLINFO_CERTINFO
'connect_time'	CURLINFO_CONNECT_TIME
'content_type'	CURLINFO_CONTENT_TYPE
'download_content_length'	CURLINFO_CONTENT_LENGTH_DOWNLOAD
'filetime'	CURLINFO_FILETIME
'header_size'	CURLINFO_HEADER_SIZE
'http_code'	CURLINFO_HTTP_CODE
'local_ip'	CURLINFO_LOCAL_IP
'local_port'	CURLINFO_LOCAL_PORT
'namelookup_time'	CURLINFO_NAMELOOKUP_TIME
'pretransfer_time'	CURLINFO_PRETRANSFER_TIME
'primary_ip'	CURLINFO_PRIMARY_IP
'primary_port'	CURLINFO_PRIMARY_PORT
'redirect_count'	CURLINFO_REDIRECT_COUNT
'redirect_time'	CURLINFO_REDIRECT_TIME
'redirect_url'	CURLINFO_REDIRECT_URL
'request_size'	CURLINFO_REQUEST_SIZE
'size_download'	CURLINFO_SIZE_DOWNLOAD
'size_upload'	CURLINFO_SIZE_UPLOAD

---

[11] curl_getinfo(): http://php.net/curl_getinfo

Key	Constant
'speed_download'	CURLINFO_SPEED_DOWNLOAD
'speed_upload'	CURLINFO_SPEED_UPLOAD
'ssl_verify_result'	CURLINFO_SSL_VERIFYRESULT
'starttransfer_time'	CURLINFO_STARTTRANSFER_TIME
'total_time'	CURLINFO_TOTAL_TIME
'upload_content_length'	CURLINFO_CONTENT_LENGTH_UPLOAD
'url'	CURLINFO_EFFECTIVE_URL

curl_getinfo does not include all values with an associated constant in the associative array it returns. In other words, there are some values you can fetch by constant and not by array. As of PHP 7, these are the documented constants to which this applies.

- CURLINFO_APPCONNECT_TIME
- CURLINFO_CONDITION_UNMET
- CURLINFO_COOKIELIST
- CURLINFO_FTP_ENTRY_PATH
- CURLINFO_HEADER_OUT
- CURLINFO_HTTPAUTH_AVAIL
- CURLINFO_HTTP_CONNECTCODE
- CURLINFO_NUM_CONNECTS
- CURLINFO_OS_ERRNO
- CURLINFO_PRIVATE
- CURLINFO_PROXYAUTH_AVAIL
- CURLINFO_RESPONSE_CODE
- CURLINFO_RTSP_CLIENT_CSEQ
- CURLINFO_RTSP_CSEQ_RECV
- CURLINFO_RTSP_SERVER_CSEQ
- CURLINFO_RTSP_SESSION_ID
- CURLINFO_SSL_ENGINES

For more information, consult the PHP manual page for curl_getinfo()[12].

---

[12] curl_getinfo(): *http://php.net/function.curl-getinfo*

Handling Headers

CURLOPT_HEADER holds a Boolean flag that, when set to `true`, causes `curl_exec()` to include headers in the response string it returns.

Another option for getting at some of the data included in the response headers—such as the HTTP response code—is to use `curl_getinfo()`, as shown in the following example.

```
$ch = curl_init();
// ...
$response = curl_exec($ch);
$info = curl_getinfo($ch);
$response_code = curl_getinfo($ch, CURLINFO_HTTP_CODE);
```

CURLOPT_HTTPHEADER holds an enumerated array of custom request header name-value pairs formatted like so.

```
$ch = curl_init();
curl_setopt($ch, CURLOPT_HTTPHEADER, [
    'Accept-Language: en-us,en;q=0.5',
    'Accept-Charset: ISO-8859-1,utf-8;q=0.7,*;q=0.7',
    'Keep-Alive: 300',
    'Connection: keep-alive'
]);
```

Debugging

`curl_getinfo()` enables you to view requests being sent by cURL. This usage can be handy when debugging. Below is an example of this feature in action.

```
$ch = curl_init();
curl_setopt_array($ch, [
    CURLOPT_RETURNTRANSFER => true,
    CURLINFO_HEADER_OUT => true
]);
curl_exec($ch);
$request = curl_getinfo($ch, CURLINFO_HEADER_OUT);
```

- CURLOPT_RETURNTRANSFER receives a value of `true` in the `curl_setopt_array()` call even though the return value of `curl_exec()` isn't captured. This prevents unwanted output.
- CURLINFO_HEADER_OUT receives a value of `true` in the `curl_setopt_array()` call to keep a copy of the request after it's sent.
- `curl_getinfo()` receives CURLINFO_HEADER_OUT to limit its return value to a string containing the kept request.

Cookies

cURL can persist cookies received from the server in memory or a local file and then use them in later requests.

Listing 4.3

```
1.  <?php
2.  $cookie_jar = '/path/to/file';
3.
4.  $ch = curl_init();
5.
6.  $url = 'http://example.com';
7.  curl_setopt($ch, CURLOPT_URL, $url);
8.  curl_setopt($ch, CURLOPT_COOKIEJAR, $cookie_jar);
9.  curl_exec($ch);
10.
11. $url = 'http://example.com/path/to/form';
12. curl_setopt($ch, CURLOPT_URL, $url);
13. curl_setopt($ch, CURLOPT_COOKIEFILE, $cookie_jar);
14. curl_exec($ch);
15.
16. curl_close($ch);
```

Here is a quick list of pertinent points.

- After the first curl_exec() call, cURL has stored the value of the Set-Cookie response header returned by the server in the file referenced by '/path/to/file' on the local filesystem as per the CURLOPT_COOKIEJAR setting. This setting value persists through the second curl_exec() call. Remember, this file and directory should be readable and writable by your PHP process.

- When the second curl_exec() call takes place, the CURLOPT_COOKIEFILE setting also points to '/path/to/file'. This causes cURL to read the contents of that file and use it as the value for the Cookie request header when constructing the request.

- If $cookie_jar contains an empty string, cookie data persists in memory rather than a local file. This behavior improves performance (memory access is faster than disk) and security (file storage may be more open to access by other users and processes than memory depending on the server environment). Note that this data persists for the life of the request (e.g., when using PHP-FPM[13] or using PHP from the command line). As such, if you require persistence beyond that, use a local file for storage rather than memory.

Sometimes, it may be desirable for the CURLOPT_COOKIEJAR value to have a different value per request, such as for debugging. In most cases, though, you set CURLOPT_COOKIEJAR for the first request to receive the initial cookie data, and its value persists for later requests.

---

[13]   PHP-FPM: http://php-fpm.org

In most cases, CURLOPT_COOKIEFILE receives the same value as CURLOPT_COOKIEJAR after the first request. This results in the request including the same cookie data and the file receiving cookie data from the response (and overwriting any existing data at that location) for use in later requests.

On a related note, if you want cURL to begin a new session to have it discard data for session cookies (i.e., cookies without an expires date), you can set the CURLOPT_COOKIESESSION setting to true.

If you want to handle cookie data manually for any reason (e.g., to be able to extract data from cookie values), you can set the value of the Cookie request header via the CURLOPT_COOKIE setting. To get access to the response headers, set the CURLOPT_HEADER and CURLOPT_RETURNTRANSFER settings to true. These settings cause the curl_exec() call to return the entire response, including the headers and the body.

Recall there is a single blank line between the headers and the body and that a colon separates each header name from its corresponding value. This information, combined with the basic string handling functions in PHP, should be all you need. Also, you'll need to set CURLOPT_FOLLOWLOCATION to false to prevent cURL from processing redirects automatically. Not doing this would cause the loss of any cookies set by requests resulting in redirects.

HTTP Authentication

cURL supports both Basic and Digest HTTP authentication methods, among others. The CURLOPT_HTTPAUTH setting controls the method to use and receives the value of one of the constants CURLAUTH_BASIC or CURLAUTH_DIGEST. The CURLOPT_USERPWD setting is a string containing the authentication credentials to use in the format 'username:password'. Note that this setting does not persist between requests; you must set it for each request requiring authentication.

```php
// Use Basic HTTP authentication...
curl_setopt($ch, CURLOPT_HTTPAUTH, CURLOPT_BASIC);

// ... or Digest HTTP authentication
curl_setopt($ch, CURLOPT_HTTPAUTH, CURLOPT_DIGEST);

// Either way, set credentials
curl_setopt($ch, CURLOPT_USERPWD, 'username:password');
```

Security

When making requests using HTTPS, it's essential to verify SSL certificates for security. This requires using a CA (Certificate Authority) bundle.

If you compile the PHP cURL extension on your system against cURL 7.10 or later, it uses a default bundle installed with the extension. Whether that bundle remains up to date or not depends on how frequently the extension receives updates.

If you would prefer to keep your bundle current without also having to update your cURL extension or be dependent on whoever maintains the package for it to update the bundle, consider using the Certainty library[14], which you can install via Composer using the package name `paragonie/certainty`. Refer to Listing 4.4.

Listing 4.4

```php
1.  <?php
2.  $fetcher = new \ParagonIE\Certainty\RemoteFetch();
3.
4.  curl_setopt_array($ch, [
5.      // Verify the peer's certificate
6.      CURLOPT_SSL_VERIFYPEER => true,
7.
8.      // Check for the existence of a common name and verify that
9.      // it matches the hostname provided
10.     CURLOPT_SSL_VERIFYHOST => 2,
11.
12.     // Use the current CA bundle provided by Certainty
13.     CURLOPT_CAINFO => $fetcher->getLatestBundle(),
14.
15.     // Verify the certificate's status;
16.     // requires PHP 7.0.7 / cURL 7.41.0
17.     CURLOPT_SSL_VERIFYSTATUS => true,
18. ]);
```

Redirection

To have cURL automatically process redirects—that is, to have it detect Location headers in server responses and implicitly issue requests until the server response no longer contains a Location header— set CURLOPT_FOLLOWLOCATION to true.

If the target application is misbehaving, it may return a Location header in every response, causing the client to get stuck in an infinite loop. cURL provides a CURLOPT_MAXREDIRS setting to prevent this, which contains an integer representing the maximum number of Location headers to be process automatically before assuming the target application is misbehaving and terminating processing.

If CURLOPT_FOLLOWLOCATION receives a value of false or curl_exec() reaches the the redirect limit defined by CURLOPT_MAXREDIRS, curl_exec() still returns true. If you set CURLOPT_RETURNTRANSFER to true, curl_exec() returns the body of the last response received before redirect processing terminating. The return value of curl_getinfo() also reflects the last response received.

To have authentication credentials persist in new requests resulting from redirects, set the CURLOPT_UNRESTRICTED_AUTH setting to true. In doing so, bear in mind the security implications: cURL may send your credentials to any URL the server specifies. Compromised servers can return URLs pointing to another server intended to steal your credentials. When sending credentials or

---

[14] Certainty library: https://github.com/paragonie/certainty

other sensitive data, consider turning off automatic processing of redirects and handling them manually to ensure you control which servers receive your information (Listing 4.5).

Listing 4.5

```php
1.  <?php
2.  // Process Location headers indefinitely. Be careful with this!
3.  curl_setopt($ch, CURLOPT_FOLLOWLOCATION, true);
4.
5.  // Process up to 5 Location headers, then terminate
6.  curl_setopt($ch, CURLOPT_FOLLOWLOCATION, true);
7.  curl_setopt($ch, CURLOPT_MAXREDIRS, 5);
8.
9.  // Persist authentication credentials when processing
10. // Location headers
11. curl_setopt($ch, CURLOPT_UNRESTRICTED_AUTH, true);
```

Referrers

CURLOPT_REFERER allows you to set the value of the Referer header explicitly. The constant name is consistent with the header name with regard to the misspelling of the word "referer."

Setting CURLOPT_AUTOREFERER (also consistent with the header misspelling) to true causes cURL to automatically set the value of the Referer header whenever it processes a Location header. See Listing 4.6.

Listing 4.6

```php
1.  <?php
2.  // Set the referrer
3.  curl_setopt($ch, CURLOPT_URL, 'http://example.com/path/to/resource');
4.  curl_setopt($ch, CURLOPT_REFERER, 'http://example.com/path/to/referrer');
5.
6.  // When processing a redirect, automatically assign to CURLOPT_REFERER the value
7.  // assigned to CURLOPT_URL in the request that initiated the redirect, and repeat
8.  // this process for any subsequent requests that result in redirects
9.  curl_setopt($ch, CURLOPT_AUTOREFERER, true);
```

Content Caching

CURLOPT_TIMECONDITION must be set to either CURL_TIMECOND_IFMODSINCE or CURL_TIMECOND_IFUNMODSINCE to select whether the If-Modified-Since or If-Unmodified-Since header is used respectively.

CURLOPT_TIMEVALUE receives the value of a UNIX timestamp (a date representation using the number of seconds between the UNIX epoch and the desired date) to represent the last client access time of the resource. You can use the \DateTime[15] class to derive this value from a timestamp.

Listing 4.7

```php
1. <?php
2. // Use an If-Modified-Since header...
3. curl_setopt($ch, CURLOPT_TIMECONDITION, CURL_TIMECOND_IFMODSINCE);
4.
5. // ... or an If-Unmodified-Since header
6. curl_setopt($ch, CURLOPT_TIMECONDITION, CURL_TIMECOND_IFUNMODSINCE);
7.
8. // Either way, set a timestamp appropriate for the selected header
9. $datetime = new \DateTime('2018-12-04T21:35:56-06:00');
10. curl_setopt($ch, CURLOPT_TIMEVALUE, $datetime->format('U'));
```

User Agents

CURLOPT_USERAGENT sets the User-Agent header value to use. For why you might want to do this, see the "User Agents" section of *Chapter 2*.

```php
// Spoof the user agent header to appear to be Internet Explorer 10
curl_setopt(
    $ch, CURLOPT_USERAGENT,
    'Mozilla/5.0 (compatible; MSIE 10.0; Windows NT 6.1; WOW64; Trident/6.0'
);
```

Byte Ranges

CURLOPT_RESUME_FROM sets a single point within the document from which to start the response body. This sets the Range header to a value of X- where X is the specified starting point.

If you wish to specify more than one range, CURLOPT_RANGE accepts a string in the same format as the Range header (ex: X-Y,Z-).

```php
// Fetch the response starting after the first kilobyte
curl_setopt($ch, CURLOPT_RESUME_FROM, '1024');

// Fetch the first kilobyte of the full response body
curl_setopt($ch, CURLOPT_RANGE, '0-1023');
```

---

[15] \Datetime: *http://php.net/datetime*

DNS Caching

You may notice code using the cURL extension appears to run faster than code using streams. cURL implements an internal DNS cache, a feature that is more prominent if your operating system or internet service provider does not provide one.

DNS, or Domain Name System, is a system used to derive an IP address for a domain name in the same way that people use phone directories to get a phone number for a person using their name. The process of obtaining an IP address for a domain name, called a DNS lookup, can be a time-consuming operation.

Because the results of DNS lookups don't change often, DNS caching is often used to keep the results of lookups for a specific period. This caching can happen at the source code level as with cURL, natively at the OS level, or via software like nscd[16] or dnsmasq[17] run either locally or on remote servers such as those used by internet service providers.

cURL enables DNS caching is by default. Some situations like debugging may warrant disabling it, which you can do by setting CURLOPT_DNS_USE_GLOBAL_CACHE to false. cURL will also by default keep the results of DNS lookups in memory for one minute. To change this, set the CURLOPT_DNS_CACHE_TIMEOUT setting to the number of seconds a result should remain in the cache before expiring.

```
// Disable cURL's DNS cache
curl_setopt($ch, CURLOPT_DNS_USE_GLOBAL_CACHE, false);

// Enable cURL's DNS cache, expire cache entries after 5 minutes
curl_setopt($ch, CURLOPT_DNS_USE_GLOBAL_CACHE, true);
curl_setopt($ch, CURLOPT_DNS_CACHE_TIMEOUT, 300); // 60 secs/minute * 5 minutes
```

Also noteworthy is the fact that cURL DNS caching is not thread-safe. Threading is a particular style of parallel processing. The most common implementation of threading consists of multiple threads of execution contained within a single operating system process that share resources such as memory.

Because of this, cURL DNS caching may operate unpredictably in a threaded environment such as Windows Server or *NIX running a threaded Apache MPM such as the worker MPM, even to the extent of causing PHP processes to crash. In PHP 7.0.2, if you attempt to use cURL DNS caching with a thread-safe version of PHP, PHP implicitly disables it and emits a warning; see PHP bug #71144[18] for more information. Newer releases appear to have fixed this bug.

If you are using the HTTP streams wrapper or any of the PHP-based HTTP client libraries covered in this book and you have access to install software on your server, you may want to install

---

[16]   nscd: https://linux.die.net/man/8/nscd
[17]   dnsmasq: http://www.thekelleys.org.uk/dnsmasq/doc.html
[18]   PHP bug #71144: https://bugs.php.net/bug.php?id=71144

a local DNS caching daemon to improve performance. Try nscd or dnsmasq on *NIX. *Chapter 8* on writing a custom HTTP client covers writing DNS caching into your client.

Timeouts

CURLOPT_CONNECTTIMEOUT is a maximum amount of time in seconds a cURL operation can attempt to make a connection. You can set it to 0 to disable this limit, but this is inadvisable in a production environment as it could leave PHP processes hanging until the target server terminates the connection from its side or an operator manually kills the processes. Note that this time includes DNS lookups. For environments where the DNS server in use or the web server hosting the target application is not responsive enough, it may be necessary to increase the value of this setting.

CURLOPT_TIMEOUT is the maximum number of seconds to limit the execution time of individual cURL extension function calls. Note that the value for this setting should include the value for CURLOPT_CONNECTTIMEOUT. In other words, CURLOPT_CONNECTTIMEOUT is a segment of the time represented by CURLOPT_TIMEOUT, so the value of the latter should be higher than the value of the former.

```php
// Allow 1 second for cURL to connect to the target server
curl_setopt($ch, CURLOPT_CONNECTTIMEOUT, 1);

// Allow 3 seconds for cURL requests to complete: CURLOPT_CONNECTTIMEOUT represents
// 1 second, leaving 2 seconds to complete after establishing the connection
curl_setopt($ch, CURLOPT_TIMEOUT, 3);
```

Basic Request Pooling

Because it's C code, the cURL extension has one feature that libraries written in PHP cannot replicate: the ability to run more than one request at a time. You can provide requests for cURL to run all at once. Then, rather than waiting to receive a response for the first request before sending the second, cURL sends all requests simultaneously and processes them as their respective servers return responses. This feature makes the time to collectively complete all requests the same as the time for the slowest individual request to complete. Take care not to overload a single host with requests when using this feature, as that server's operators may interpret it as an attempted denial of service (DoS) attack.

Listing 4.8 shows a simple example which waits until all requests have completed before attempting to process them.

Listing 4.8

```php
1. <?php
2. $ch1 = curl_init('http://example.com/resource1');
3. curl_setopt($ch1, CURLOPT_RETURNTRANSFER, true);
4. // ...
5.
```

```
 6. $ch2 = curl_init('http://example.com/resource2');
 7. curl_setopt($ch2, CURLOPT_RETURNTRANSFER, true);
 8. // ...
 9.
10. $mh = curl_multi_init();
11. curl_multi_add_handle($mh, $ch1);
12. curl_multi_add_handle($mh, $ch2);
13.
14. $running = null;
15. do {
16.     curl_multi_exec($mh, $running);
17. } while ($running > 0);
18.
19. $ch1_response = curl_multi_getcontent($ch1);
20. $ch2_response = curl_multi_getcontent($ch2);
21.
22. curl_multi_remove_handle($mh, $ch1);
23. curl_close($ch1);
24.
25. curl_multi_remove_handle($mh, $ch2);
26. curl_close($ch2);
27.
28. curl_multi_close($mh);
```

1. Initialize and configure two session handles $ch1 and $ch2 as normal. Note that you can use more than two handles in this manner; but two serves the purpose of this example.

2. Initialize a multi handle $mh using curl_multi_init()[19].

3. Add the two session handles to the multi handle using curl_multi_add_handle()[20].

4. Use a loop in conjunction with a flag $running to check (i.e., poll) the multi handle for completion of all contained requests.

5. curl_multi_getcontent()[21] gets the response bodies of the two session handles.

6. Remove the session handles from the multi handle and close it using curl_multi_remove_handle()[22] and curl_close()[23], respectively.

7. Close the multi handle using curl_multi_close()[24].

---

[19] curl_multi_init(): *http://php.net/curl_multi_init*
[20] curl_multi_add_handle(): *http://php.net/curl_multi_add_handle*
[21] curl_multi_getcontent(): *http://php.net/curl_multi_getcontent*
[22] curl_multi_remove_handle(): *http://php.net/curl_multi_remove_handle*
[23] curl_close(): *http://php.net/curl_close*
[24] curl_multi_close(): *http://php.net/curl_multi_close*

More Efficient Request Pooling

Listing 4.9 examines how to process requests as soon as they return, even while processing other requests or waiting for them to process.

Listing 4.9

```php
1.  <?php
2.  $requests = [];
3.
4.  $ch1 = curl_init();
5.  // ...
6.  $requests[] = $ch1;
7.
8.  $ch2 = curl_init();
9.  // ...
10. $requests[] = $ch2;
11.
12. // ...
13.
14. $window_size = 4;
15. $timeout = 1;
16.
17. $callback = function($output, $info) {
18.     // ...
19. };
20.
21. $request_count = count($requests);
22. if ($request_count < $window_size)
23.     $window_size = $request_count;
24.
25. $master = curl_multi_init();
26. for ($i = 0; $i < $window_size; $i++)
27.     curl_multi_add_handle($master, $requests[$i]);
28.
29. do {
30.     while (($execrun = curl_multi_exec($master, $running)) == CURLM_CALL_MULTI_PERFORM) {
31.         // intentionally empty body
32.     }
33.
34.     // if we encounter an error, terminate the outer loop
35.     if ($execrun != CURLM_OK)
36.         break;
37.
```

```
38.    // One or more requests were just completed, for each one...
39.    while ($done = curl_multi_info_read($master)) {
40.
41.        // Send the corresponding response data to the processing callback
42.        $output = curl_multi_getcontent($done['handle']);
43.        $info = curl_getinfo($done['handle']);
44.        call_user_func($callback, $output, $info);
45.
46.        // Start the next request in the list
47.        if (isset($requests[$i])) {
48.            curl_multi_add_handle($master, $requests[$i]);
49.            $i++;
50.        }
51.
52.        // Remove the cURL handle for the request that was just processed
53.        curl_multi_remove_handle($master, $done['handle']);
54.    }
55.
56.    // Block until the state of active requests changes or a timeout is reached
57.    if ($running) {
58.        curl_multi_select($master, $timeout);
59.    }
60. } while ($running);
61.
62. curl_multi_close($master);
```

- Add pre-configured cURL handles to the array $requests.
- Set $window_size to limit the number of requests sent simultaneously, generally to 2, 4, 6, or 8 to mimic most browsers. This is a control measure to reduce the likelihood of this code executing a DoS attack.
- Set $timeout to the amount of time in seconds to wait between completed requests before polling for newly completed requests. This limits CPU usage of the PHP process executing the script and should generally be a floating point number between 0 and 1 (exclusive).
- $callback is a closure used to process individual requests as they complete. It accepts two parameters: $output is a string that contains the response body and $info is an associative array that contains other metadata about the response.
- If the number of requests in $requests is less than $window_size, set the latter to the former. In that event, queue all requests in the initial batch.
- Add cURL handles for the initial batch of requests, up to $window_size, to the multi handle.
- Start a loop and maintain it while any requests in the current batch are still executing or requests are remaining outside the current batch waiting to execute.
- Within the loop, when a request completes, get its response body and metadata and pass them to $callback.

- Add the cURL handle for the next request to execute to the multi handle, then remove the cURL handle for the completed request from the multi handle.
- Block the loop until one of the requests in the current batch has activity or runs for a number of seconds equal to $timeout, then repeat the process.
- Once all requests execute, exit the loop and close the multi handle.

Libraries

If you would rather not roll your own, there are libraries which wrap the cURL functionality for sending parallel requests in a more user-friendly API, such as chuyskywalker/rolling-curl[25] and the PECL extension reviewed in the next chapter. Search for "curl" on packagist.org[26] for more options.

[25] chuyskywalker/rolling-curl: https://github.com/chuyskywalker/rolling-curl
[26] packagist.org: https://packagist.org

Chapter

5

pecl_http Extension

The pecl_http extension[1] first became available in PHP 5. The extension's 1.x branch has since reached end-of-life, is no longer supported, and is not covered in this book. The extension's second major version targets PHP 5.3 and, among other significant API changes, uses the namespaces feature introduced in that release. A third major version was later released for interoperability with PHP 7, with limited changes to the second version's API that affected compatibility; see the extension changelog[2] for more information.

Like the cURL extension, the pecl_http extension also wraps the libcurl library and has similar advantages as a result, such as its internal DNS cache. While the cURL extension uses resources and configuration options to mimic libcurl's API, the pecl_http extension offers the same features in the form of an object-oriented API. As a result, code using pecl_http is generally shorter than code using the cURL extension.

---

[1]   pecl_http extension: _https://mdref.m6w6.name/http_
[2]   the extension changelog: _https://phpa.me/pecl-http-changelog_

Another major difference is the cURL extension is part of the PHP core, which means it's more often than not present in most environments supporting PHP. pecl_http is not, and thus may not be present or available in shared hosting environments depending on the hosting provider, which may be a concern for code distributed for use in a variety of environments.

Installation

The pecl_http extension may be available through your OS package manager. Package names can vary (e.g., php5-pecl-http for Debian-based Linux distributions), and may lag the current stable version of the extension, but this is generally the most straightforward installation option.

Another option is installing pecl_http via the PECL installer which requires installation of PEAR[3]. A package for PEAR may also be available through your OS package manager (e.g., php-pear for Debian-based Linux distributions).

After installing the PECL installer, issue the command pecl install pecl_http, or to install manually from source, download the latest version[4].

Installation requires the header files for the PHP version you are using. You can find these in the PHP source tarballs available for download[5] or possibly also through your OS package manager (e.g., php5-dev for Debian-based Linux distributions). Also required are the header files for the libcurl library, which may also be available through your OS package manager (e.g., libcurl4-openssl-dev for Debian-based Linux distributions).

To confirm the availability of the pecl_http extension with shell access to the server, you can run php -m and look for an instance of http in the output. You can consult the output any of the following function calls from within a PHP script.

```
// inspect php output
phpinfo(\INFO_MODULES);
// inspect array of extensions
var_export(get_loaded_extensions());
// test if a http_* function exists
var_dump(function_exists('http_get'));
```

GET Requests

Listing 5.1 is an example of issuing a simple GET request.

---

[3]   installation of PEAR: http://pear.php.net/installation
[4]   download the latest version: http://pecl.php.net/get/pecl_http
[5]   download: http://www.php.net/downloads.php

Listing 5.1

```php
1. <?php
2. $request = new \http\Client\Request('GET', 'http://example.com');
3. $client = new \http\Client;
4. $client->enqueue($request, function(\http\Client\Response $response) {
5.     var_dump($response->getResponseCode(),
6.              $response->getHeaders(),
7.              (string) $response->getBody());
8. });
9.
10. $client->send();
```

- The \http\Client\Request class represents requests. Its constructor takes four parameters. The first two shown here are the request method to use ('GET' in this case) and the target URL. The two optional parameters which follow are an associative array mapping HTTP request header names to their corresponding values and an instance of \http\Message\Body that contains data for the request body, which the next section discusses further.

- The \http\Client class represents the HTTP client. This example instantiates the class and calls its enqueue() method to queue the request with a callback to process the response. The callback takes an instance of the response class \http\Client\Response as its one argument. The client's send() method then sends all queued requests.

POST Requests

Now let's look at how to perform a POST request.

Listing 5.2

```php
1. <?php
2. $data = [ 'param1' => 'value1',
3.           'param2' => 'value2' ];
4.
5. $files = [
6.     [ 'name' => 'file1',
7.       'type' => 'image/jpeg',
8.       'file' => '/path/to/file1.jpg' ],
9.     [ 'name' => 'file2',
10.       'type' => 'image/gif',
11.       'file' => '/path/to/file2.gif' ]
12. ];
13.
14. $body = new \http\Message\Body;
15. $body->addForm($data, $files);
16. $request = new \http\Client\Request(
17.     'POST', 'http://example.com', null, $body
18. );
```

```
19.
20. $client = new \http\Client;
21. $client->enqueue( $request, function(\http\Client\Response $response) {
22.     // ...
23. });
24. $client->send();
```

- The \http\Message\Body class represents the request body. Its addForm() method adds both key-value pairs and file data to the request body. Either parameter can be explicitly set to null to exclude it.

- As with GET requests, the \http\Client\Request class represents POST requests. The first constructor parameter for the request method receives a value of 'POST' this time, followed by the URL as in the previous example. The third parameter for headers receives a value of null which allows specifying $body for the fourth parameter.

- What follows is identical to the previous GET request example: instantiate \http\Client, call its enqueue() method with $request and the callback to process the response, and then call its send() method to fire off the request.

Request Options

Request options control features; this section details how to set them. Later sections describe which request options control these features and what their associated values are to avoid repeating the information in this section.

The \http\Client\Request class has a setOptions() method to receive request options in the form of an associative array mapping options to their respective values. We must call this method before queueing the request for transmission. See Listing 5.3.

Listing 5.3

```
1.  <?php
2.  $options = ['option_name' => 'option_value'];
3.
4.  $request = new \http\Client\Request('GET', 'http://example.com');
5.  $request->setOptions($options);
6.
7.  // ...
8.
9.  $client = new \http\Client;
10. $client->enqueue($request, function(\http\Client\Response $response) {
11.     // ...
12. });
13. $client->send();
```

For a list of available request options, see *"Options" section* of the documentation for the \http\Client\Curl namespace.

Handling Headers

You can set more than one request header at once using an associative array with header names for keys pointing to corresponding header values. This usage contrasts with the cURL extension, which uses an enumerated array of string values, each containing one header name-value pair.

```
$headers = [
    'User-Agent' => 'Mozilla/5.0 (X11; U; ...',
    'Connection' => 'keep-alive'
];
```

The \http\Client\Request and \http\Client\Response classes extend \http\Message, which provides methods for dealing with headers for requests and responses alike. You can set request headers can using the third parameter of the constructor for \http\Client\Request or its setHeader() and setHeaders() methods. The addHeader() and addHeaders() methods append to headers that can take more than one value.

Listing 5.5

```php
1.  <?php
2.  // sets request headers via constructor
3.  $request = new \http\Client\Request('GET', 'http://example.com', $headers);
4.
5.  // sets request headers, overwriting any existing header values
6.  $request->setHeader('Referer', 'http://other.example.com');
7.  $request->setHeaders($headers);
8.
9.  // sets request headers, appending to any existing header values
10. $request->addHeader('Cookie', 'foo=bar');
11. $request->addHeaders([ 'Cookie' => 'baz=bay',
12.                        'Access-Control-Request-Method' => 'GET' ]);
13.
14. // accesses existing header values
15. echo $request->getHeader('Referer');
16. var_dump($request->getHeaders());
17.
18. $client = new \http\Client;
19. $client->enqueue($request, function(\http\Client\Response $response) {
20.     // accesses response header values
21.     echo $response->getHeader('Date');
22.     var_dump($response->getHeaders());
23. });
24. $client->send();
```

Debugging

\http\Message, the parent class of \http\Client\Request and \http\Client\Response, implements the magic method __toString(). When you treat a request or response object as a
string—such as passing it to echo—the __toString() method is implicitly invoked and returns the
request or response in string form.

Listing 5.6

```
1.  <?php
2.  $request = new \http\Client\Request(
3.     'GET', 'http://google.com', ['Content-Type' => 'application/html']
4.  );
5.  echo $request;
6.
7.  $client = new \http\Client;
8.  $client->enqueue( $request, function(\http\Client\Response $response) {
9.     echo $response;
10. });
11. $client->send();
```

Timeouts

As with cURL, pecl_http uses a common set of request options for handling timeouts.

The 'timeout' request option, which corresponds to CURLOPT_TIMEOUT, is the maximum number
of seconds an entire request may take before timing out.

Likewise, the 'connecttimeout' request option, the counterpart for CURLOPT_CONNECTTIMEOUT, is
the number of seconds a connection attempt, which includes DNS resolution, may take. DNS resolution and connection times are part of the entire request time, so the value of 'timeout' should be
greater than the value of 'connecttimeout'.

The 'dns_cache_timeout' request option, which functions like CURLOPT_DNS_CACHE_TIMEOUT, is the
number of seconds to keep a DNS cache entry and defaults to 120 seconds (two minutes).

Content Encoding

If you are unfamiliar with content encoding, see _Content Encoding_ in Chapter 8 for more information. To enable it when using pecl_http, set the 'compress' request option to true.

Note that this requires libz support. You can check for this by executing the phpinfo() function
within a PHP script and looking in the section for the HTTP extension or by running php --ri http
from the command line. If libz support is on, output like the example below (specifically the last line)
should be present. Otherwise, you can use the technique detailed in Chapter 8 for handling encoded
content in the response.

```
http

HTTP Support => enabled
Extension Version => 2.5.6

Used Library => Compiled => Linked
libz => 1.2.5 => 1.2.5
```

Cookies

You can send, receive, and persist cookies with the pecl_http extension similarly as with the cURL extension.

Listing 5.7

```php
1.  <?php
2.  $requestCookies = [ 'foo' => 'foovalue',
3.                      'bar' => 'barvalue' ];
4.
5.  $cookieJar = '/path/to/cookiejar';
6.
7.  $options = [ 'cookies' => $requestCookies,
8.               // or
9.               'cookiestore' => $cookieJar,
10.              // and optionally
11.              'encodecookies' => false,
12.              'cookiesession' => true, ];
13.
14. $request = new \http\Client\Request('GET', 'http://example.com');
15. $request->setOptions($options);
16.
17. $client = new \http\Client;
18. $client->enqueue($request, function (\http\Client\Response $response) {
19.    $parsed = new \http\Cookie($response->getHeader('Set-Cookie'));
20.    var_dump($parsed->getCookie('cookie-name'), $parsed->getCookies());
21. });
22.
23. $client->send();
```

Request options are available for handling cookies:

- 'cookies' sources cookie data from an associative array
- 'cookiestore' sources cookie data from a file
- 'encodecookies' controls whether cookie data is URL-encoded before sending it
- 'cookiesession' controls whether to ignore session cookies loaded from a file

To access cookie values in responses, within the callback to process the response, get the value of the Set-Cookie header using the getHeader() method of $response, then instantiate \http\Cookie and pass the header value to its constructor. The getCookie() and getCookies() methods of this object return the string value of an individual cookie or an associative array of cookies values keyed by cookie name respectively.

HTTP Authentication

The 'httpauth' request option sets credentials and takes a string in the format 'username:password' for its value.

The 'httpauthtype' request option, which takes its value from one of the http\Client\Curl::AUTH_* constants[6], controls the authentication type used.

You can set the 'unrestricted_auth' request option to true to include authentication credentials in requests resulting from redirects pointing to a different host from the current one. To maintain control over which servers receive the credentials, keep this option set to false and process redirects manually.

Here is an example of how to perform a GET request using basic HTTP authentication.

```
$request = new \http\Client\Request('GET', 'http://example.com');
$request->setOptions([
    'httpauth' => 'username:password',
    'httpauthtype' => \http\Client\Curl::AUTH_BASIC,
    'unrestricted_auth' => false,
]);
$request->send();
```

Redirection and Referrers

The 'redirect' request option sets the number of redirects to process before automatically terminating. This option defaults to 0, which disables processing of redirects, and you must explicitly set this request option to a value greater than 0 to enable it. If you're sending authentication credentials or other sensitive data, consider handling redirects manually to control which servers receive that information.

The 'referer' request option sets the value of the Referer request header. You can also set it via the 'headers' request option mentioned earlier in this chapter.

---

[6]   constants: *https://phpa.me/pecl-http-auth-type*

Content Caching

The 'lastmodified' request option takes a UNIX timestamp to use as the value for the If-Modified-Since or If-Unmodified-Since request header.

Likewise, the 'etag' request option accepts a string to use as the value for the If-Match or If-None-Match request header.

> *Determining which headers the* lastmodified *and* etag *options use is not clear and can change if you include a* Range *header. You may need to experiment to find which settings work with a particular host.*

User Agents

The 'useragent' request option sets a custom user agent string for the request. *Chapter 2* explains why and when you should set a custom one.

Byte Ranges

Like cURL, pecl_http includes request options for a resume point and byte ranges. The former is 'resume' and accepts an integer for the starting point. The latter is 'range' and takes an array of enumerated arrays each containing a pair of integers representing a single byte range. What follows is an example of setting byte ranges within a request options array.

```
$options = [
    'range' => [
        [0, 1023], // first 1024 bytes (1 KB)
        [3072, 4095], // fourth 1024 bytes (1 KB)
    ]
];
```

You can also set byte ranges using custom headers, such as with the 'headers' request option.

```
$options = [
    'headers' => [
        'Range' => 'bytes=0-1023,3072-4095',
    ]
];
```

Request Pooling

pecl_http also inherits cURL's support for request pooling, or sending and processing requests in parallel. Like other features, pecl_http implements it more succinctly (see Listing 5.8). To queue more than one request, call the enqueue() method of \http\Client once for each request object.

Listing 5.8

```php
<?php
$request1 = new \http\Client\Request('GET', 'http://localhost1.example');
$request2 = new \http\Client\Request('GET', 'http://localhost2.example');

$callback = function(\http\Client\Response $response) {
    // ...
};

$client = new \http\Client;
$client->enqueue($request1, $callback);
$client->enqueue($request2, $callback);
$client->send();
```

Chapter

6

Guzzle

In late February 2012, Michael Dowling released the Guzzle HTTP client[1] library under the MIT License. It would go on to power the Amazon Web Services SDK client library for PHP as well as version 8 of the Drupal content management system. Like the pecl_http extension, Guzzle aimed to simplify using the cURL extension while not impeding its power. Over time, it has developed into a robust and popular HTTP client library, including support for using PHP streams in environments where the cURL extension is not available.

One notable trait of Guzzle is it supports the PSR-7 standard[2] created by the PHP Framework Interop Group (PHP-FIG). PSR-7 defines interfaces for HTTP messages usable by both clients and servers.

At the time of this writing, the current stable Guzzle release is version 6. It requires PHP 5.5 and the cURL extension compiled with libcurl 7.19.4+ including OpenSSL and zlib support. Installing

---

[1]   Guzzle HTTP client: http://docs.guzzlephp.org
[2]   PSR-7 standard: http://www.php-fig.org/psr/psr-7/

Guzzle via Composer automatically downloads all other dependencies; see the Guzzle installation directions[3] for more information.

Simple Request and Response Handling

Let's perform a single GET request using Guzzle.

```php
$client = new \GuzzleHttp\Client;
$response = $client->get('http://example.com');
$body = (string) $response->getBody();
```

- Create an instance of \GuzzleHttp\Client. Its constructor takes an optional parameter not specified here: an associative array of options used by all requests created by the client.
- The get() method of the client executes the request synchronously and returns an instance of a class that implements the PSR-7 interface \Psr\Http\Message\ResponseInterface, in this case, GuzzleHttp\Psr7\Response.
- The getBody() method of the response returns an instance of a class that implements the PSR-7 interface \Psr\Http\Message\StreamInterface, such as \GuzzleHttp\Psr7\Stream or \GuzzleHttp\Psr7\PumpStream. Typecasting this object to a string returns the data from the HTTP response body.

POST Requests

POST requests look like GET requests but require use of the post() method and one more parameter to specify request body data.

```php
$response = $client->post('http://example.com', [
    'form_params' => [
        'field_1' => 'value_1',
        'field_2' => 'value_2',
        // ...
    ],
]);
```

Specifying the 'form_params' request option automatically handles adding a Content-Type request header of application/x-www-form-urlencoded and applying URL encoding to the specified field values.

Uploading a file requires a different request option, as shown in Listing 6.1.

---

[3]   Guzzle installation directions: *https://phpa.me/guzzlephp-installation*

Listing 6.1

```php
1.  <?php
2.  $response = $client->post(
3.      'http://example.com', [
4.      'multipart' => [
5.          [
6.              'name' => 'field_1',
7.              'contents' => 'value_1',
8.              // request options below are optional
9.              'filename' => 'filename.txt',
10.             'headers' => [
11.                 'X-Header' => 'header-value',
12.             ],
13.         ],
14.         [
15.             'name' => 'field_2',
16.             'contents' => fopen('/path/to/file', 'r'),
17.         ],
18.     ],
19. ]);
```

The 'multipart' option is an enumerated array of associative arrays. Each associative array must contain the keys 'name', the value of which is a string containing the name of the field, and 'contents', which can contain either a string, a PHP stream resource representing the file contents, or an instance of a class implementing the PSR-7 StreamInterface interface[4].

Handling Headers

There may be cases when you need to specify custom request headers, such as when specifying a pre-formatted request body or a custom user agent string.

```php
$response = $client->post( 'http://example.com', [
    'body' => 'field_1=value_1&field_2=value_2',
    'headers' => [
        'Content-Type' => 'application/x-www-form-urlencoded',
        'User-Agent' => 'My User Agent 1.0',
    ],
]);
```

Here, the 'body' option specifies the request body. The 'headers' option is an associative array of header names mapped to their respective values. Here, it manually adds the Content-Type header—which is automatically added when using the 'form_params' option—and sets a custom User-Agent header value.

---

[4]   PSR-7 StreamInterface interface: https://www.php-fig.org/psr/psr-7/#13-streams

Response headers are collectively accessible from the getHeaders() method of the response object, which returns an associative array mapping header names to their respective values. Headers are individually accessible using one of two methods: getHeaderLine() and getHeader(). The difference between them is their return types, which are string and array respectively.

In most cases, you probably want to use getHeaderLine(). If a header has a single value, this method returns that value as a string. For headers with more than one value, it returns those values as a comma-delimited string.

getHeader() is useful in cases where a header may have more than one value, and it's useful to deal with them as an array of strings. Note that this method always returns an array, even if a header has a single value.

You can find more details about how PSR-7 implementations handle headers in section 1.2 of the specification.

Analyzing Responses

The response object exposes the response status code and corresponding reason phrase via its getStatusCode() and getReasonPhrase() methods respectively. In the rare instance you need the HTTP protocol version, use the getProtocolVersion() method to get it.

Handling Large Files

You may encounter cases where the response body is large and you need to siphon it to an external source, such as a file, to avoid loading all the data into memory at once.

You can approach this in two ways. The first method is simple: pass a stream resource as the value of the 'sink' request option, and Guzzle writes the response body to that stream.

```php
$client->get('http://example.com', ['sink' => fopen('path/to/file', 'w')]);
```

The second method is more complex but provides more fine-grained control of the download process. It uses the PSR-7 StreamInterface instance returned by the response object's getBody() method shown in Listing 6.2.

Listing 6.2

```php
1. <?php
2. $response = $client->get('http://example.com');
3. $body = $response->getBody();
4. $file = fopen('path/to/file', 'w');
5.
6. while (!$body->eof()) {
7.     $chunk = $body->read(1024);
8.     fwrite($file, $chunk);
9. }
10.
11. fclose($file);
```

- Rather than typecasting the return value of getBody() to a string—as in the earlier example—it's assigned to the variable $body as-is.
- A writable stream is opened to the file path/to/file and assigned to the variable $file.
- The eof() method of $body determines whether the data stream ends. If not, the while loop continues.
- The read() method of $body reads a 1,024 byte or 1 kilobyte chunk of the data stream and assigns it to the variable $chunk, which is subsequently appended to the file represented by the $file stream.
- When the data stream ends, the eof() method of $body returns true, thus terminating the while loop and closing the $file stream.

Handling Errors

By default, responses with a status code in the 400 or 500 ranges result in throwing an exception. To suppress this behavior, set the 'http_errors' request option to false.

For more information, see the Guzzle manual section on the 'http_errors' option[5].

Request Objects

Previous examples have performed a request and retrieved the response in a single call. It's also possible to instantiate and configure a request object before sending the request.

```
$request = new \GuzzleHttp\Psr7\Request(
    'POST',
    'http://example.com',
    ['Content-Type' => 'application/x-www-form-urlencoded'],
    'field_1=value_1&field_2=value_2'
);
$response = $client->send($request);
```

The above example functions identically to the first example from the earlier "Handling Headers" section of this chapter. Here are the differences:

- Instead of indicating the request method by the function called on the client object, it's specified as a string and passed as the first parameter to the Request constructor.
- The Request constructor receives the URL for the request as the second parameter, rather than the client method receiving it as its first parameter.
- The third and fourth Request constructor parameters are for the request headers and the request body, where they would otherwise be request options within the second client method parameter.
- The client object's send() method receives the request, sends it, and returns the response.

---

[5]   'http_errors' *option:* *https://phpa.me/guzzlephp-opts-http-errors*

- While not used in this example, the send() method takes a second parameter: an associative array of request options that, in previous examples, is the second parameter to the client method corresponding to the request method.

Connectivity

Guzzle provides request options for terminating a request at different points if it exceeds the timeout threshold. Each of these options takes a floating-point number value representing the number of seconds to wait.

- 'connect_timeout' represents the time to establish an initial connection to the server.
- 'timeout' represents the time to begin to receive a response from the server. This includes the time represented by 'connect_timeout'.
- 'read_timeout' represents the time to read data from a streamed response body (when the 'stream' request option is enabled).

Debugging

Guzzle provides a handy function which returns the contents of both request and response objects; this is indispensable for debugging.

Listing 6.3

```php
1. <?php
2. use GuzzleHttp\Client;
3. use GuzzleHttp\Psr7\Request;
4. use function GuzzleHttp\Psr7\str;
5.
6. $client = new Client;
7. $request = new Request('GET', 'https://example.com');
8. $response = $client->send($request);
9.
10. echo str($request), PHP_EOL;
11. echo str($response), PHP_EOL;
```

The output of Listing 6.3 should look like the following.

```
GET / HTTP/1.1
Host: example.com

HTTP/1.1 200 OK
Date: Sat, 04 Nov 2017 15:08:12 GMT
Expires: -1
Cache-Control: private, max-age=0
Content-Type: text/html; charset=ISO-8859-1

[body]
```

Guzzle also supports a 'debug' request option analogous to cURL's CURLOPT_VERBOSE constant. We can send debugging output to STDOUT.

```
$response = $client->get('https://example.com', ['debug' => true]);
```

We can also send debug output to a writable directory.

```
$response = $client->get('https://example.com',
                    ['debug' => fopen('path/to/log', 'w')]);
```

Cookies

As with cURL, Guzzle implements the concept of a "cookie jar" for persisting cookies set between requests.

The simplest use case for cookies is to have the client receive them in responses, store them, and then include them in later requests. To do this, set the 'cookies' request option to true when instantiating the client.

```
$client = new \GuzzleHttp\Client(['cookies' => true]);
```

To access cookie data from a specific request, pass an instance of the \GuzzleHttp\Cookie\CookieJar class as the value of the 'cookies' option for that request.

```
$jar = new \GuzzleHttp\Cookie\CookieJar;
$response = $client->get('https://example.com', ['cookies' => $jar]);
```

You can also do this when instantiating the client to make all cookie data from the client session accessible.

```
$jar = new \GuzzleHttp\Cookie\CookieJar;
$client = new \GuzzleHttp\Client(['cookies' => $jar]);
```

Within the cookie jar object, Guzzle represents each cookie as an instance of the \GuzzleHttp\Cookie\SetCookie class. The jar object itself is an iterable collection of these objects and also supports fetching them individually by cookie name.

Listing 6.4

```php
1. <?php
2. foreach ($jar as $cookie) {
3.     echo $cookie->getName();
4.     echo $cookie->getValue();
5.     echo $cookie->getDomain();
6.     echo $cookie->getPath();
7.     echo $cookie->getMaxAge();
8.     echo $cookie->getExpires();
9.     echo $cookie->getSecure();
10.    echo $cookie->getDiscard(); // true if this is a session cookie
11.    echo $cookie->getHttpOnly();
12.    $cookieArray = $cookie->toArray();
13. }
14.
15. $fooCookie = $jar->getCookieByName('foo');
16.
17. $cookiesArray = $jar->toArray();
```

For more information, see the Guzzle manual section on cookies[6] and the section on the 'cookies' request option[7].

Redirection

By default, Guzzle automatically handles processing up to five redirects. You can change this behavior using the 'allow_redirects' request option. The following example shows how to disable redirects.

```php
// Disable automatic redirect processing
$client = new \GuzzleHttp\Client(['allow_redirects' => false]);
```

You can also adjust the limit when creating a new client instance.

```php
// Enable automatic redirect processing, but reduce quantity to 3
$client = new \GuzzleHttp\Client([
    'allow_redirects' => [
        'max' => 3,
    ],
]);
```

For more information, see the Guzzle manual section on the 'allow_redirects'[8] request option.

---

[6]   cookies: https://phpa.me/guzzlephp-cookies
[7]   request option: https://phpa.me/guzzlephp-opts-cookies
[8]   'allow_redirects': https://phpa.me/guzzlephp-opts-redirects

Authentication

Guzzle supports both Basic and Digest HTTP authentication with the `'auth'` request option.

Listing 6.5

```php
1. <?php
2. // Basic
3. $response = $client->get( 'https://example.com', [
4.     'auth' => ['username', 'password']
5. ]);
6.
7. // Digest
8. $response = $client->get( 'https://example.com', [
9.     'auth' => ['username', 'password', 'digest']
10. ]);
```

If you specify a username and password, Guzzle assumes it should use Basic authentication.

If you instead pass the string `'digest'` as the third array element, Guzzle uses Digest authentication. Note that support for this is presently limited to environments in which Guzzle uses cURL.

For more information, see the Guzzle manual section on the `'auth'`[9] request option.

Security

When making requests over SSL using HTTPS, it's essential for security to verify SSL certificates as valid. This verification uses a CA (Certificate Authority) bundle file.

By default, Guzzle attempts verification by checking in common locations for the CA bundle to use, but this won't work on all systems.

If you know the location of a pre-existing bundle file on your system, you can specify the path to it explicitly using the `'verify'` Guzzle request option.

```php
$client = new \GuzzleHttp\Client(['verify' => 'path/to/cert.pem']);
```

If you would prefer to use a more global setting for the CA bundle path instead of using the `'verify'` request option, you can do so in your PHP INI configuration. Guzzle checks the `openssl.cafile` setting first and uses it where available. If Guzzle is using cURL, you can also use the `curl.cainfo` setting, which Guzzle checks second.

For more information on the `'verify'`[10] request option, refer to its section in the Guzzle manual.

---

[9] `'auth'`: *https://phpa.me/guzzlephp-opts-auth*
[10] `'verify'`: *https://phpa.me/guzzlephp-opts-verify*

If you do not know the location of your CA bundle or do not already have a process in place to ensure it stays up-to-date, consider using the Certainty library[11], which you can install via Composer using the package name paragonie/certainty.

```
$fetcher = new \ParagonIE\Certainty\RemoteFetch();
$client = new \GuzzleHttp\Client(['verify' => $fetcher->getLatestBundle()]);
```

The above example downloads a current CA bundle to your local filesystem. By default, it checks for updates to the bundle once per day.

If you want to change the frequency of updates or the location of the bundle, or for other usages of Certainty, consult the Certainty documentation[12].

Asynchronous Requests

Examples thus far have used synchronous requests, which block further execution of the PHP process until the request terminates. Guzzle also supports asynchronous requests, which allow execution of the PHP process to continue while requests are still in transit.

Invocation of asynchronous requests differs from that of synchronous requests in two major ways. The first difference is the method which invokes the request has an Async suffix. The example below calls getAsync() rather than get(). The parameters passed to the getAsync() method are the same as those passed to get().

```
$promise = $client->getAsync('https://example.com');
```

The other significant difference is the client returns a promise object rather than returning a response. The Promises/A+ specification[13] describes the concept of promises in more detail. Guzzle implements this specification in the form of the guzzlehttp/promises library[14].

In short, a promise represents a value that is determined in the future. In this case, it represents the response that the client will receive. In the example above, the promise is an instance of a class that implements the \GuzzleHttp\Promise\PromiseInterface interface, such as \GuzzleHttp\Promise\FulfilledPromise or \GuzzleHttp\Promise\RejectedPromise.

One of two outcomes can occur with a promise:

1. The request succeeds, and the client receives a response.
2. The request fails, and the client throws an exception.

   Promises provide the ability to specify callbacks to handle both of these outcomes.

---

[11]   *Certainty library: https://github.com/paragonie/certainty*
[12]   *Certainty documentation: https://phpa.me/paragonie-certainty-docs*
[13]   *Promises/A+ specification: https://promisesaplus.com*
[14]   guzzlehttp/promises *library: https://github.com/guzzle/promises*

Listing 6.7

```php
1.  <?php
2.  use GuzzleHttp\Exception\RequestException;
3.  use Psr\Http\Message\ResponseInterface;
4.
5.  $promise->then(
6.      function (ResponseInterface $response) {
7.          // The request succeeded, do something useful with the response here
8.      },
9.      function (RequestException $exception) {
10.         // The request failed, handle it here
11.         echo $exception->getMessage();
12.
13.         // To get the request that caused the exception, do this
14.         $request = $exception->getRequest();
15.     }
16. );
```

The then() method of the promise object takes two parameters: one callback to handle the response if the request succeeds and another callback to handle the exception if the request fails. Note, both of these parameters are optional and you may omit them or skip them by specifying null as their respective values.

One useful aspect of then() is it returns a promise object. This feature allows you to chain calls to then(), where the value received by the success handler of a given then() call is the value returned by the success handler of the previous then() call in the chain.

Listing 6.8

```php
1.  <?php
2.  $client = new \GuzzleHttp\Client;
3.  $promise = $client->getAsync('https://example.com');
4.  $promise->then(
5.      function (ResponseInterface $firstResponse) use ($client) {
6.          $body = (string) $firstResponse->getBody();
7.
8.          // Assuming that $body contains a URL, extract that URL into a variable $url
9.          // Validate that the value of $url appears to be legitimate for security
10.         return $client->getAsync($url);
11.     }
12. )->then(
13.     function (ResponseInterface $secondResponse) {
14.         // Do something useful with the second response here
15.     }
16. );
```

The example in Listing 6.8 invokes an asynchronous request. The promise returned by the client for that request is then configured with two callbacks using two chained calls to then().

When the client receives the response, it invokes the success callback passed to the first then() call and passes it the response object $firstResponse. The callback then extracts a URL from the response body and invokes another asynchronous request for the extracted URL. The client likewise returns a promise for this second request.

This returned promise resolves to a value internally. This value is subsequently passed as $secondResponse to the success callback specified in the second then() call above.

Concurrent Requests

As well as supporting asynchronous execution of requests, Guzzle also supports executing requests concurrently.

Listing 6.9

```php
1. <?php
2. $client = new \GuzzleHttp\Client;
3. $promises = [
4.     $client->getAsync('https://example.com/1'),
5.     $client->getAsync('https://example.com/2'),
6.     $client->getAsync('https://example.com/3'),
7.     $client->getAsync('https://example.com/4'),
8. ];
9.
10. // Throws an exception if any of the requests fail.
11. $responses = \GuzzleHttp\Promise\unwrap($promises);
12.
13. // Waits for all requests to complete, even if any of them fail.
14. $responses = \GuzzleHttp\Promise\settle($promises)->wait(true);
15.
16. // Assuming all requests complete, access responses like this.
17. // Array keys correspond to those used in $promises
18. $firstResponse = (string) $responses[0]->getBody();
19. $secondResponse = (string) $responses[1]->getBody();
20. // ...
```

Chapter

7

Zend Framework

Zend Framework (often abbreviated ZF) launched in 2005, and the second major version saw its first release in late 2012. The last version of the older 1.x branch, ZF 1.12.20, requires PHP 5.2.11. The ZF 2.5 release split the framework into separate components with different versions and release cycles. The latest version of the HTTP client component as of this writing, 2.9.1, requires PHP 5.6 or higher; examples in this chapter use this version.

> Note: In 2019, the Zend Framework project became the Laminas[1] project. At the time of this writing, no code releases are available, but apart from updating namespaces for ZF2, the code here should work the same.

Designed to take full advantage of the new object system introduced in PHP 5, ZF has a fully object-oriented API. In particular, ZF2 takes advantage of the namespaces support added in PHP

---

[1]   Laminas: https://getlaminas.org

5.3. The project team strives to maintain an E_STRICT level of compliance and comprehensive code coverage via unit testing.

Among the components included in ZF are Zend\Http\Client[2] in ZF2 and Zend_Http_Client[3] in ZF1, HTTP client libraries with feature sets equivalent to the others already covered in previous chapters.

With that, let's move on to how these libraries work.

Basic Requests

Let's start with a basic GET request.

```
// ZF1
$client = new Zend_Http_Client;
$client->setUri('http://example.com');
$response = $client->request();
```

- We pass the URL for the request to the setUri() method.
- The request() method of the client dispatches the request and returns a response. It takes an optional parameter of a string containing the HTTP request method to use and uses 'GET' by default.

See the example below for another way to use the ZF1 API[4].

```
// ZF1
$client = new Zend_Http_Client('http://example.com');
$response = $client->request('GET');
```

This example functions identically to the previous one, with these differences:

- Rather than specifying the URL for the request using the setUri() method, it's specified when instantiating the client. This behavior is primarily useful when using the client object to make a single request.
- 'GET' is explicitly passed to request() as the HTTP request method to use.

An alternative way to set the HTTP request method involves calling the client's setMethod() method and passing it a constant value representing the desired request method, as in the example below.

```
// ZF1
$client->setMethod(Zend_Http_Client::GET);
```

---

[2]   Zend\Http\Client: *https://docs.zendframework.com/zend-http/*
[3]   Zend_Http_Client: *https://phpa.me/zf1-zend-http*
[4]   ZF1 API: *https://phpa.me/zf1-http*

The ZF2 API[5] is similar. As mentioned, it uses namespaces, with a base namespace of Zend\Http. It has a Client class and a Request class.

Here's an example of a simple GET request.

```
// ZF2
$request = new Zend\Http\Request;
$request->setUri('http://example.com');
$client = new Zend\Http\Client;
$response = $client->dispatch($request);
```

- In this example, the setUri() method of the Request instance receives the request URI.
- The client's dispatch() method dispatches the Request instance and returns the response.

As in ZF1, ZF2 allows you to pass the request URL to the client using its setUri() method.

```
// ZF2
$client->setUri('http://example.com');
```

Another option is to pass the URL to the constructor.

```
// ZF2
$client = new Client('http://example.com');
```

To set the HTTP request method in ZF2, call the setMethod() method of the request object with a constant value representing the desired request method.

```
// ZF2
$request->setMethod(Request::METHOD_GET);
```

Setting query string parameters for a request in ZF1 looks like this.

```
// ZF1
$client->setParameterGet([
    'param1' => 'value1',
    'param2' => 'value2',
    // ...
]);
```

Note this applies to both GET and POST requests.

---

[5]   ZF2 API: https://phpa.me/zf2-http-client

Speaking of POST requests, here's what one looks like in ZF1.

```
// ZF1
$client->setMethod(Zend_Http_Client::POST);
$client->setParameterPost([
    'param1' => 'value1',
    'param2' => 'value2',
]);
```

The example above calls the setMethod() of the request object with Request::METHOD_POST rather than Request::METHOD_GET.

Likewise, setParameterPost() adds variable-value pairs to the request body. Unlike setParameterGet(), setParameterPost() does not apply to GET requests.

By default, data added to the request body in this way has an application/x-www-form-urlencoded MIME type, the default type used by HTML forms. You can set data with a different type like this.

```
// ZF1
$client->setRawData($xmlString, 'text/xml');

// This does the same thing
$client->setRawData($xmlString)->setEncType('text/xml');
```

ZF2 uses a different approach. It has a library apart from its HTTP client, zendframework/zend-stdlib. This library contains an interface, Zend\Stdlib\ParametersInterface, which extends PHP core interfaces including ArrayAccess, Countable, and Traversable. An implementation of that interface, Zend\Stdlib\Parameters, is also included; it's based on the PHP ArrayObject class. Zend\Http\Request uses this to store both query string parameters and request body parameters, which are accessible via its getQuery() and getPost() methods respectively.

```
// ZF2
$request->setMethod(Request::METHOD_POST);
```

These method calls all set a query string parameter value.

```
$request->getQuery()->param1 = 'value1';
$request->getQuery()['param1'] = 'value1';
$request->getQuery()->set('param1', 'value1');
$request->getQuery()->offsetSet('param1', 'value1');
```

These access a query string parameter value.

```
echo $request->getQuery()->param1;
echo $request->getQuery()['param1'];
echo $request->getQuery('param1');
echo $request->getQuery()->offsetGet('param1');
```

Likewise, these set a request body parameter value.

```
$request->getPost()->param1 = 'value1';
$request->getPost()['param1'] = 'value1';
$request->getPost()->set('param1', 'value1');
$request->getPost()->offsetSet('param1', 'value1');
```

And these method calls return a request body parameter value.

```
echo $request->getPost()->param1;
echo $request->getPost()['param1'];
echo $request->getPost('param1');
echo $request->getPost()->offsetGet('param1');
```

For more on basic requests in ZF1, see *Introduction—Zend_Http*[6]. For ZF2, see Zend\Http\Request *Quick Start*[7].

Responses

In ZF1, the response object returned by the client's request() method, which is an instance of the Zend_Http_Response class, has useful accessor methods. The abstraction this provides makes code using this library more readable than, say, using cURL directly.

getStatus() returns an integer containing the status code.

```
var_dump($response->getStatus());
```

getMessage() returns a string containing a description for the status code.

```
var_dump($response->getMessage());
```

getBody() returns a string containing the fully decoded response body.

```
var_dump($response->getBody());
```

getRawBody() returns a string containing the unaltered response body.

```
var_dump($response->getRawBody());
```

getHeaders() returns an associative array of headers.

```
var_dump($response->getHeaders());
```

getHeader() returns a string or array of values for a single header.

```
var_dump($response->getHeader('Content-Type'));
```

---

[6]   *Introduction—Zend_Http:* https://phpa.me/zf1-http-client
[7]   Zend\Http\Request *Quick Start:* https://phpa.me/zf2-http-request-start

isSuccessful() returns true for 100- and 200-level status codes.

```
var_dump($response->isSuccessful());
```

isError() returns true for 400- and 500-level status codes.

```
var_dump($response->isError());
```

The response object in ZF2 has similar methods, though most have different names. Its getHeaders() method returns an instance of \Zend\Http\Headers, which has more useful methods for accessing information.

getStatusCode() returns an integer containing the status code.

```
var_dump($response->getStatusCode());
```

getReasonPhrase() returns a string containing a description for the status code.

```
var_dump($response->getReasonPhrase());
```

getBody() returns a string containing the fully decoded response body.

```
var_dump($response->getBody());
```

getContent() returns a string-castable value containing the unaltered response body.

```
var_dump((string) $response->getContent());
```

Chaining toArray() on getHeaders() returns an associative array of headers.

```
var_dump($response->getHeaders()->toArray());
```

Calling get() on getHeaders() returns a string or array of values for a single header.

```
var_dump($response->getHeaders()->get('Content-Type'));
```

Each of these methods returns TRUE for a range of status codes.

```
var_dump($response->isInformational()); // 1XX
var_dump($response->isSuccessful());    // 2XX
var_dump($response->isRedirect());      // 3XX
var_dump($response->isClientError());   // 4XX
var_dump($response->isServerError());   // 5XX
```

For more on handling responses in ZF1, see Zend_Http_Response[8]. For ZF2, see Zend\Http\Response[9].

---

[8]   Zend_Http_Response: *https://phpa.me/zf1-http-response*
[9]   Zend\Http\Response: *https://phpa.me/zf2-http-response*

URL Handling

In ZF1, by default, `Zend_Http_Client` uses `Zend_Uri_Http` for validation of any URI passed into the client. Use of unconventional URLs, like those using characters described as disallowed by section 2.4.3 of RFC 2396[10] (the predecessor to RFC 3986), may cause validation failure. See the following code sample for how to deal with this situation.

Check if a URI or URL is valid with `check()`. Here, `$valid` is `false` because the URL contains a |.

```
$valid = Zend_Uri::check('http://example.com/?q=this|that');
```

The static `setConfig()` method forces URLs with disallowed characters to pass validation. Now, `$valid` is `true` because `'allow_unwise'` is enabled.

```
Zend_Uri::setConfig(['allow_unwise' => true]);
$valid = Zend_Uri::check('http://example.com/?q=this|that');
```

The following method call returns to the default behavior so that URLs with disallowed characters no longer pass validation.

```
Zend_Uri::setConfig(['allow_unwise' => false]);
```

ZF2 URI validation is less strict and does not have this issue.

For more information on this in ZF1, see *Using Zend_Http_Client*[11].

Custom Headers

The `setHeaders()` method is the Swiss Army Knife of header management for ZF1's `Zend_Http_Client` class. See the example below for the multitude of ways for setting headers.

You can set a single header by passing a header name and value as separate arguments.

```
$client->setHeaders('Host', 'example.com');
```

You can set a single header by passing a header name and value together as a string argument.

```
$client->setHeaders('Host: example.com');
```

`setHeaders()` can set a single header with more than one value, mainly useful for cookies.

```
$client->setHeaders('Cookie', [ 'lang=en-US',
                                'PHPSESSID=1a0b82148815944c548caef5ccb884c9',]);
```

---

[10]   RFC 2396: *https://www.rfc-editor.org/rfc/rfc2396.txt*
[11]   Using Zend_Http_Client: *https://phpa.me/zf1-http-client-usage*

You can pass headers as an array of key-value pairs with header names and values separate.

```
$client->setHeaders([ 'Host' => 'example.com',
                      'User-Agent' => 'Zend_Http_Client 1.7.2' ]);
```

You can also pass headers as an array of strings, with header names and values together.

```
$client->setHeaders([ 'Host: example.com',
                      'User-Agent: Zend_Http_Client 1.7.2' ]);
```

In ZF2, both \Zend\Http\Request and \Zend\Http\Response have getHeaders() and setHeaders() methods which handle an instance of \Zend\Http\Headers, which offers the same functionality as Zend_Http_Client->setHeaders() and more.

Again, you can set a single header by passing a header name and value as separate arguments to addHeaderLine().

```
$headers->addHeaderLine('Host', 'example.com');
```

Or, call addHeaderLine() to set a single header by passing the header name and value together.

```
$headers->addHeaderLine('Host: example.com');
```

You can set a single header with more than one value as an array passed as the second argument, which is mainly useful for setting cookies.

```
$headers->addHeaderLine('Cookie', ['lang=en-US',
                      'PHPSESSID=1a0b82148815944c548caef5ccb884c9',]);
```

Call addHeaders() to set headers, with header names and values as separate key-value pairs.

```
$headers->addHeaders([ 'Host' => 'example.com',
                       'User-Agent' => 'Zend_Http_Client 1.7.2', ]);
```

You can also pass header names and values together by passing an array of strings to addHeaders().

```
$headers->addHeaders([ 'Host: example.com',
                       'User-Agent: Zend_Http_Client 1.7.2', ]);
```

For more on handling headers in ZF1, see *Setting Custom Request Headers*[12]. For ZF2, see the Headers class[13] documentation.

---

[12]   *Setting Custom Request Headers*: *https://phpa.me/zf1-client-custom-headers*
[13]   the Headers *class*: *https://phpa.me/zf2-http-headers*

Configuration

Both ZF1's `Zend_Http_Client` and ZF2's `\Zend\Http\Client` have configuration settings much like the context options of the HTTP streams wrapper, configuration settings of the cURL extension, and request options of the pecl_http extension. As shown in the examples below, settings are an associative array of name-value pairs that you can pass either as the second parameter to the class constructor or later via `Zend_Http_Client->setConfig()` or `\Zend\Http\Client->setOptions()`.

The syntax for ZF1 is as follows.

```
$config = ['timeout' => 30];

// ZF1
$client = new Zend_Http_Client('http://example.com', $config);
// or
$client->setConfig($config);
```

For ZF2 the syntax is below.

```
$config = ['timeout' => 30];

// ZF2
$client = new \Zend\Http\Client('http://example.com', $config);
// or
$client->setOptions($config);
```

Later sections of this chapter elaborate on the more relevant configuration settings.

For all available options in ZF1, see `Zend_Http_Client` configuration parameters[14]. For ZF2, see HTTP Client configuration[15].

Connectivity

The `'timeout'` configuration setting is an integer value specifying the number of seconds for which the client should attempt to connect to the server before timing out. In the event of a timeout, the client will throw an instance of the ZF1 exception `Zend_Http_Client_Adapter_Exception` or ZF2 exception `\Zend\Http\Client\Adapter\Exception\TimeoutException`.

By default, the client assumes that you are performing one request on the connection established. That is, it automatically includes a `Connection` header with a value of `close`. If you are sending more than one request to the same host, set the `keepalive` configuration to `true` to have all requests sent on the same connection for improved performance.

---

[14] *Zend_Http_Client configuration parameters: https://phpa.me/zf1-http-client-config*
[15] *HTTP Client configuration: https://phpa.me/zf2-http-client-config*

Debugging

In ZF1, you can get the last request sent by the client as a string via the getLastRequest() method. For the last response received, call the corresponding method getLastResponse(). This method returns an instance of Zend_Http_Response rather than a string. To convert this object to a string, call its asString() method. See below for examples of both.

```
// ZF1
$requestString = $client->getLastRequest();
$responseObject = $client->getLastResponse();
$responseString = $responseObject->asString();
```

Note that the 'storeresponse' configuration setting affects how getLastResponse() behaves. When set to true (the default), it stores the last response received by the client for later retrieval. When set to false, the response is not stored but is available as the return value of the client's request() method. In this case, getLastResponse() returns null. If you don't need the availability of the response, turning this off can reduce resource usage.

ZF2 works slightly differently. You can access objects for the last request sent and the response received, which are instances of \Zend\Http\Request and \Zend\Http\Response respectively, by calling the getRequest() and getResponse() methods on the client. You can get raw strings for the same by calling the getLastRawRequest() and getLastRawResponse() methods. As with ZF1, the 'storeresponse' configuration setting controls whether the client stores the last raw response. There's no corresponding setting for the request.

```
// ZF2
$requestObject = $client->getRequest();
$responseObject = $client->getResponse();
$requestString = $client->getLastRawRequest();
// works if 'storeresponse' is true, otherwise returns null
$responseString = $client->getLastRawResponse();
```

Cookies

The ZF1 Zend_Http_Client class accepts manually specified cookie name-value pairs via its setCookie() method. It will not automatically keep response cookies and resend them in later requests by default. To have it do so, call setCookieJar() with no parameters. This causes implicit instantiation of an instance of the default cookie handling class, Zend_Http_CookieJar, to be implicitly instantiated.

If you need access to cookie data for something other than propagating it to later requests, there are ways to do so. Cookies are accessible individually via the cookie jar's getCookie() method, the required parameters for which are a URI and a cookie name.

```
// ZF1
$client->setCookieJar();

$cookie = $client->getCookieJar()
                ->getCookie('http://example.com/', 'cookiename');
```

Note that the URI includes a scheme (http://), a domain (example.com), and a path (/). A single cookie jar instance can store cookie data for more than one domain and more than one path on the same domain. In cases not using the latter capability, specify the root path / so all cookies set on the domain are available to all paths under that domain. The getMatchingCookies() method of Zend_Http_CookieJar allows collective access to cookies based on these criteria and returns an array of Zend_Http_Cookie objects by default. See below for examples.

```
// ZF1

// All cookies for the domain example.com
$cookies = $cookiejar->getMatchingCookies('http://example.com/');

// All cookies for the domain example.com with a path or subpath of /some/path
$cookies = $cookiejar->getMatchingCookies('http://example.com/some/path');

// All non-session cookies for the domain example.com
$cookies = $cookiejar->getMatchingCookies('http://example.com/', false);
```

You can use getAllCookies() to access all cookies contained in the cookie jar instance. When using a cookie jar to store cookies for a single domain, getAllCookies() offers a more concise method than getMatchingCookies() to retrieve all cookies for that domain. Like getMatchingCookies(), getAllCookies() also returns an array of Zend_Http_Cookie objects by default.

The ZF2 Zend\Http\Client class accepts cookie data via its addCookie(), addCookies(), and setCookies() methods. addCookie() accepts a pre-URL-encoded string or an instance of the Zend\Http\Header\SetCookie class while addCookies() and setCookies() accept arrays of elements of either type. addCookie() can also take two parameters, the unencoded name and value for a single cookie.

Note when using Zend\Http\Header\SetCookie it assumes the provided cookie value is not encoded by default. To use a pre-encoded value, call the setEncodeValue() method on the relevant instance of Zend\Http\Header\SetCookie and pass it a value of false as shown in the example below.

Call the addCookie() method to set a cookie as either two arguments for a name value, or a string with an equal sign (=) separating the name and value.

```
$client->addCookie('name', 'unencoded value');
$client->addCookie('name=encoded%20value');
```

You can create the header and pass it to addCookie(). If the value is already encoded, make sure to call setEncodeValue() to false.

```php
$header = new \Zend\Http\Header\SetCookie('foo', 'bar');
$client->addCookie($header);

$header = new \Zend\Http\Header\SetCookie('foo2', 'encoded%20value');
$header->setEncodeValue(false);
$client->addCookie($header);
```

Last, you can pass an array of string with name-value pairs to either addCookies() or setCookies().

```php
$cookies = [ 'name1=encoded%20value%201',
             'name2=encoded%20value%202', ];

$client->addCookies($cookies);
// or
$client->setCookies($cookies);
```

You can also persist cookies returned in a response in later requests. The code to do this is more explicit (Listing 7.1).

Listing 7.1

```php
1. <?php
2. // ZF2
3.
4. $cookies = new Zend\Http\Cookies;
5.
6. $client->setUri('http://...');
7. $response = $client->request('GET');
8. $cookies->addCookiesFromResponse($response, $client->getUri());
9.
10. $client->setUri('http://...');
11. $client->addCookies($cookies->getMatchingCookies($client->getUri()));
12. $response = $client->request('GET');
```

To access cookies outside of persisting them, the getCookie() and getAllCookies() methods complement the getMatchingCookies() method used in the above example.

To access all cookies, you can do the following.

```
$cookies = new \Zend\Http\Cookies;

// Returns an array of instances of Zend\Http\Header\SetCookie
$all = $cookies->getAllCookies();

// Same as above
$all = $cookies->getAllCookies(Cookies::COOKIE_OBJECT);
```

The first argument to getAllCookies() controls how it returns cookies. This example returns an array of strings, each corresponding to a single cookie and containing a valid value for a Set-Cookie HTTP header.

```
$asStrings = $cookies->getAllCookies(Cookies::COOKIE_STRING_ARRAY);
```

Using Cookies::COOKIE_STRING_CONCAT returns a single string corresponding to all cookies containing a valid value for a Set-Cookie HTTP header.

```
$asString = $cookies->getAllCookies(Cookies::COOKIE_STRING_CONCAT);
```

You can also access individual cookies. This returns an instance of Zend\Http\Header\SetCookie.

```
$myCookie = $cookies->getCookie($client->getUri(), 'cookie_name');

// Same as above
$myCookie = $cookies->getCookie(
    $client->getUri(), 'cookie_name', Cookies::COOKIE_OBJECT
);
```

This returns a single string containing a valid value for a Set-Cookie HTTP header for cookie_name.

```
$myCookie = $cookies->getCookie(
    $client->getUri(), 'cookie_name', Cookies::COOKIE_STRING_ARRAY
);

// Same as above
$myCookie = $cookies->getCookie(
    $client->getUri(), 'cookie_name', Cookies::COOKIE_STRING_CONCAT
);
```

> ### Zend\Http\Client\Cookies
>
> *In versions of ZF2 as recent as 2.2.5, a* Zend\Http\Client\Cookies *class exists which bears significant resemblance to the* Zend\Http\Cookies *class.* Zend\Http\Client\Cookies *is a deprecated residual from ZF1; do not use it. In any instance where you see the documentation reference it, assume it should reference* Zend\Http\Cookies *instead.*

Redirection

In ZF1 and ZF2, the 'maxredirects' configuration setting is an integer indicating the number of redirects to perform before terminating. Its default value is five. Upon termination, the client returns the last response it received. The isRedirect() method of the ZF1 Zend_Http_Response and ZF2 Zend\Http\Response classes returns true for responses with a 300-level status code.

Subsections 6.4.2 and 6.4.3 of RFC 7231 show when redirection occurs, the next request should use the same method and parameters. In practice, most clients don't behave this way. Instead, they revert the method to GET and clear parameters. For consistency with other clients, the ZF1 Zend_Http_Client and ZF2 Zend\Http\Client classes behave this way by default. To force either to be compliant with the RFC, set the 'strictredirects' configuration setting to true.

User Agents

The 'useragent' configuration setting contains the user agent string to use and defaults to 'Zend_Http_Client' in ZF1 and Zend\Http\Client in ZF2. *Chapter 2* explains why and when you should set a custom one.

HTTP Authentication

Both Zend_Http_Client in ZF1 and Zend\Http\Client in ZF2 support Basic HTTP authentication. To set credentials for Basic HTTP authentication in either version, call the client's setAuth() method and pass in the username and password.

```
$client->setAuth('username', 'password');
```

Zend\Http\Client in ZF2 also supports Digest HTTP authentication as of version 2.4 if its cURL adapter is in use.

```
$client = new Client([
    'adapter' => new \Zend\Http\Client\Adapter\Curl,
]);

$client->setAuth('username', 'password', Client::AUTH_DIGEST);
```

Chapter

8

Rolling Your Own

Before proceeding, it's generally better to use and build upon an existing library rather than trying to roll one from scratch. For one thing, you can get features "for free" with no work required on your part. For another, developers outside of your team and projects work on those libraries, and in the words of Eric S. Raymond, "Given enough eyes, all bugs are shallow."

That said, it certainly doesn't hurt to be familiar with this information even if you don't plan to build your own client. Doing so gives you more capability to troubleshoot issues with existing libraries and contribute patches back to their project teams.

Whatever your motivation, let's get started.

Sending Requests

As detailed in _Chapter 3_, the streams extension has wrappers for specific protocols, such as the HTTP protocol. It also offers socket transports for dealing with data at a lower level. One of these socket transports is for TCP, or Transmission Control Protocol, which is a core internet protocol used to ensure reliable delivery of an ordered sequence of bytes. The socket transport facilitates sending a raw data stream to a server, in this case, a manually constructed HTTP request.

```
$stream = stream_socket_client('tcp://example.com:80');
$request = "GET / HTTP/1.1\r\nHost: example.com\r\n\r\n";
fwrite($stream, $request);
echo stream_get_contents($stream);
fclose($stream);
```

The output of this code resembles the example below.

```
HTTP/1.1 200 OK
Host: example.com
Connection: close
X-Powered-By: PHP/7.0.18
Content-type: text/html; charset=UTF-8

Hello world!
```

- `stream_socket_client()`[1] establishes a connection with the server, returning a connection handle resource assigned to `$stream`.
- `'tcp://'` specifies the transport to use.
- `'example.com'` is the hostname of the server.
- `':80'` specifies the port on which to connect to the server. This example uses 80 because it's the standard port for HTTP. The port to use depends on the configuration of the web server.
- `$request` contains the request to send to the server. A CRLF sequence (see the Chapter 2 section on *GET Requests*) separates individual lines and the request ends with a double CRLF sequence (effectively a blank line). Note that the request *must* contain the ending sequence, or the server will hang waiting for the rest of the request.
- `fwrite()`[2] transmits the request over the established connection represented by `$stream`.
- `stream_get_contents()`[3] reads all available data from the connection; in this case, the response to the request.
- `fclose()`[4] terminates the connection explicitly.

Depending on the nature and requirements of the project, you may not know all facets of a request at one time. In this situation, you can encapsulate request metadata in a data structure such as an associative array or an object. From this, you can use a central unit of logic to read that metadata and construct a request in the form of a string based on it.

---

[1]   `stream_socket_client()`: *http://php.net/stream_socket_client*

[2]   `fwrite()`: *http://php.net/fwrite*

[3]   `stream_get_contents()`: *http://php.net/stream_get_contents*

[4]   `fclose()`: *http://php.net/fclose*

Manually constructing requests within a string as shown in the example above also doesn't have ideal readability. If you have exact requests ahead of time that do not vary, an alternative approach is storing them in a data source of some type, then retrieving them at runtime and sending them over the connection as they are. Whether it's possible to take this approach depends on the level of variance in requests going between the web scraping application and the target application.

If the need arises to build query strings or URL-encoded POST request bodies manually, http_build_query()[5] allows doing this using associative arrays.

Listing 8.1

```php
1. <?php
2. $post_data = [
3.     'param1' => 'value1',
4.     'param2' => 'value2',
5. ];
6.
7. $stream = stream_socket_client('tcp://example.com:80');
8. $request = "POST / HTTP/1.1\r\n"
9.             . "Host: example.com\r\n\r\n"
10.            . http_build_query($post_data);
11. fwrite($stream, $request);
12. $response = stream_get_contents($stream);
13. fclose($stream);
14.
15. echo $response;
```

Listing 8.1 produces output like this.

```
HTTP/1.1 411 Length Required
Content-Type: text/html
Content-Length: 357
Connection: close
Date: Tue, 18 Jun 2019 19:26:12 GMT
Server: ECSF (dcb/7F3B)

<?xml version="1.0" encoding="iso-8859-1"?>
<!DOCTYPE html PUBLIC "-//W3C//DTD XHTML 1.0 Transitional//EN"
        "http://www.w3.org/TR/xhtml1/DTD/xhtml1-transitional.dtd">
<html xmlns="http://www.w3.org/1999/xhtml" xml:lang="en" lang="en">
        <head>
                <title>411 - Length Required</title>
        </head>
        <body>
                <h1>411 - Length Required</h1>
        </body>
</html>
```

[5]   http_build_query(): http://php.net/http_build_query

Parsing Responses

Once you've received a response, the next step is extracting the data you need from it. Taking the response from the last example, let's examine what this might look like.

Listing 8.2

```php
1.  <?php
2.  // Split the headers and body into separate variables
3.  list($headers, $body) = explode("\r\n\r\n", $response, 2);
4.
5.  // Remove the status line from the headers
6.  list($status, $headers) = explode("\r\n", $headers, 2);
7.
8.  // Parse the headers segment into individual headers
9.  preg_match_all(
10.     "/(?P<name>[^:]+): (?P<value>[^\r]+)(?:$|\r\n[^ \t]*)/U",
11.     $headers,
12.     $headers,
13.     PREG_SET_ORDER
14. );
```

Logic to separate individual headers must account for the ability of header values to span more than one line as per RFC 7230 Subsection 3.2.4. As such, this example uses preg_match_all()[6] to separate individual headers. See *Chapter 15* for more information on regular expressions. If a situation necessitates parsing data contained in URLs and query strings, check out parse_url()[7] and parse_str()[8]. As with the request, it's generally desirable to parse response data into a data structure for ease of reference.

Transfer-Encoding

Before parsing the body, examine the headers. If a Transfer-Encoding header is present with a value of chunked, it means the server is sending the response back in chunks rather than all at once. The advantage to this is the server doesn't wait to compose the entire before returning it (to determine and include its length in the Content-Length header). Doing so can increase server throughput.

Before each chunk, there is a hexadecimal number indicating the size of the chunk followed by a CRLF sequence. A CRLF sequence also denotes the end of each chunk. A chunk size of zero (0) denotes the end of the body, which is important when using a persistent connection since the client must know where one response ends and the next begins.

---

[6]   preg_match_all(): *http://php.net/preg_match_all*
[7]   parse_url(): *http://php.net/parse_url*
[8]   parse_str(): *http://php.net/parse_str*

You can use strstr()[9] to get characters in a string preceding a newline. To convert strings containing hexadecimal numbers to their decimal equivalents, use hexdec()[10]. See below for an example of what these two might look like in action. The example assumes the request body is in string form.

Listing 8.3

```
1. <?php
2. $unchunked = '';
3. do {
4.     if ($length = hexdec(strstr($body, "\r\n", true))) {
5.         $body = ltrim(strstr($body, "\r\n"));
6.         $unchunked .= substr($body, 0, $length);
7.         $body = substr($body, $length + 2);
8.     }
9. } while ($length > 0);
```

See Subsection 4.1 and Appendix A.1.3 of RFC 7230 for more information on chunked transfer encoding.

Content Encoding

If the zlib extension is available (which you can check using extension_loaded()[11] or executing php -m from the command line), the client can optionally include an Accept-Encoding header with a value of gzip,deflate in its request. If the server supports content compression, it includes a Content-Encoding header in its response with a value indicating which of the two compression schemes it used on the response body before sending it.

Using compression reduces the amount of data transmitted. This, in turn, reduces bandwidth consumption and increases throughput, assuming compression and decompression take less time than data transfer, which is generally the case. Upon receiving the response, the client must decompress the response using the original scheme used by the server to compress it.

```
// If Content-Encoding is gzip...
$decoded = gzinflate(substr($body, 10));

// If Content-Encoding is deflate...
$decoded = gzuncompress($body);
```

---

[9]   strstr(): *http://php.net/strstr*
[10] hexdec(): *http://php.net/hexdec*
[11] extension_loaded(): *http://php.net/extension_loaded*

Yes, the function names are correct. One would think that gzinflate()[12] would decode a body encoded using the deflate encoding scheme. Apparently, this is an oddity in the naming scheme used by the zlib library.

When the encoding scheme is gzip, the response includes a GZIP header. gzinflate() does not respond well to this. Hence, you must strip out the header (contained in the first 10 bytes of the body) before passing the body gzinflate().

See RFC 7230 Subsection 4.2 for more information on content encoding. RFC 1951 covers specifics of the DEFLATE algorithm, the basis of the deflate encoding scheme, while RFC 1952 details the gzip file format, the basis of the gzip encoding scheme.

Timing

Each time a web server receives a request, it creates or reuses a separate line of execution in the form of a process or thread to deal with that request. Left unchecked, a large request load could consume all resources on a server. As such, web servers generally restrict the number of requests they can handle concurrently. The server blocks requests beyond this limit until it completes an existing request for which it had already allocated resources. Requests left unserved too long time out.

A denial-of-service attack describes a client overloading a server with requests to the point where it consumes the available resource pool and thereby delays or prevents the processing of requests, potentially including requests the client itself sent last. It's desirable to avoid this behavior for two reasons: 1) it's construed as abuse and the server may throttle traffic (i.e., limiting the number of further requests you can send) or block traffic from your IP; 2) it prevents the client from being consistently functional.

According to browserscope.org[13], most modern mainstream web browsers establish a limit of six concurrent connections per domain name when loading a given resource and its dependencies. As such, this is a good starting point for testing the load of the server hosting the target application. When possible, measure the response times of individual requests and compare that to the number of concurrent requests sent to determine how much of a load the server can withstand. Note that this applies to idempotent request methods such as GET, HEAD, and OPTIONS, but not to non-idempotent methods such as POST.

Depending on the application, real-time interaction with the target application may not be necessary. Specifically, it may be possible to retrieve data as necessary, cache it locally, store modifications locally, and push them to the target application in bulk during hours of non-peak usage. To discern what these hours are, observe response times during different times of day that you make requests, and locate the periods during which response times are consistently highest.

---

[12] gzinflate(): *http://php.net/gzinflate*
[13] *browserscope.org: https://www.browserscope.org*

Chapter

9

Tidy Extension

At this point, you should have completed the retrieval phase of the web scraping process and have your raw response body ready and awaiting analysis. Congratulations on making it to the halfway mark!

While other response formats are undoubtedly possible, chances are good you are dealing with a markup-based language like HTML or XHTML. As such, this chapter and later chapters deal specifically with those formats. More often than not, HTML is the language in use.

XML-focused PHP extensions are available that can deal with markup; chapters that follow this one review these. While these extensions do provide some support for HTML and are even somewhat forgiving about malformed markup, well-formed XHTML is their ideal input. The first step in the analysis process is to perform any necessary cleanup on the response body to reduce issues you may encounter later during analysis.

This chapter covers the PHP Tidy extension[1], which wraps the HTML Tidy library[2]. While the latter had a significant lull in updates around 2008, there was a resurgence of interest in 2015 when

---

[1]   PHP Tidy extension: http://php.net/tidy
[2]   HTML Tidy library: http://tidy.sourceforge.net/#docs

the World Wide Web Consortium (W3C) established an official community group for the project. Version 5.0 of the library, the first to support HTML5, was subsequently released.

Packaged releases of PHP 7 and above generally have a Tidy extension that uses a 5.x release of the HTML Tidy library. If you need to determine which release your installation is using, consult the Tidy section in either the console output of `php -i` or the output of invoking `phpinfo()` within a PHP script.

Validation

Because correcting markup malformations can add some overhead, documents you are analyzing should undergo validation to determine if such corrections are necessary.

The W3C provides a markup validation service[3] to promote adherence to web standards. It accepts markup to test by URL, file upload, or direct input. This service indicates what issues, if any, your document has with markup malformation.

Let's look at an example (Listing 9.1) of such a document.

Listing 9.1

```
1.  <!doctype html>
2.  <html>
3.      <head>
4.          <title>Foo</title>
5.      </head>
6.      <body>
7.          <table
8.              <tr>
9.                  <td>foo</td>
10.             </tr>
11.         </table>
12.     </body>
13. </html>
```

This is a simple HTML5 document with a minor error: the opening `table` tag is missing its closing `>` bracket. When the W3C validator evaluates this document, it returns an error message to this effect.

```
Error: Saw < when expecting an attribute name. Probable cause: Missing > immediately
before.
At line 8, column 7
```

Now that the sorts of malformations you may encounter when analyzing retrieved pages have been established, let's move on to how to correct those malformations.

---

[3]   markup validation service: http://validator.w3.org

Tidy

You can clean up markup malformations in two ways. One is manual, involves the use of simple string manipulation functions or regular expression functions, and can become messy and rather unmanageable. The other is more automated and involves using the Tidy extension to locate and correct markup issues. While the process is configurable, it lacks the fine-grained control that comes with handling it manually.

The majority of this chapter focuses on using Tidy to correct markup issues. For those issues Tidy cannot handle to your satisfaction, the approach mentioned earlier involving string and regular expression functions is your alternative. _Chapter 15_ covers regular expressions in more detail.

The Tidy extension offers two API styles: procedural and object-oriented. Both offer similar functionality (this chapter covers relevant differences later). Which API you use is a matter of preference. Though both API styles use objects of the tidy class, use one style for the sake of consistency in syntax. Code examples in this chapter show both styles.

Input

Before correcting markup issues in a set of markup data, you must parse the data into a tidy object. More often than not, markup data is already contained within a string or an external file when it's ready for parsing. See below for an example of how to handle either of these cases. The next section covers the configuration represented by the $config variable.

You can use tidy's functionality procedurally.

```
$tidy = tidy_parse_string($string, $config);
$tidy = tidy_parse_file($filename, $config);
```

You can also use it through an object-oriented API.

```
$tidy = new tidy;
$tidy->parseString($string, $config);
$tidy->parseFile($filename, $config);
```

Configuration

Like the cURL extension, the Tidy extension operates mainly on the concept of configuration; hence, $config parameters are present in all calls in the above example. Unlike most other extensions, you can provide this parameter in two forms: an associative array of setting-value pairs or the path to an external configuration file.

The configuration file format is akin to individual style settings in a CSS stylesheet. It's unlikely a non-developer needs to access the configuration settings and not the PHP source code using Tidy as well. As such, separation into an external configuration file is useful for the sake of not cluttering source code with settings. The configuration file being from disk may pose performance concerns when in high use.

Here is an example of what a Tidy configuration[4] file might look like:

```
// single-line comment
/* multi-line comment */
indent: false /* setting: value */
wrap: 78
```

A configuration array corresponding to the above example would look like this:

```
$config = [
    'indent' => false,
    'wrap' => 78,
];
```

When using the object-oriented API, an alternative to using configuration files is subclassing the tidy class and overriding its parseString() and parseFile() methods to automatically include specific configuration setting values. This approach allows for easy reuse of Tidy configurations, as in Listing 9.2.

Listing 9.2

```
1.  <?php
2.  class mytidy extends tidy
3.  {
4.      private $_default = ['indent' => false,
5.                           'wrap' => 78 ];
6.
7.      public function parseFile($filename, $config, $encoding, $use_include_path = false)
8.      {
9.          return parent::parseFile( $filename,
10.                                    array_merge($this->_default, $config),
11.                                    $encoding,
12.                                    $use_include_path);
13.     }
14.
15.     public function parseString($filename, $config, $encoding, $use_include_path=false)
16.     {
17.         return parent::parseString( $filename,
18.                                     array_merge($this->_default, $config),
19.                                     $encoding,
20.                                     $use_include_path);
21.     }
22. }
```

---

[4]   Tidy configuration: *https://phpa.me/tidy-quickref*

- `array_merge()`[5] consolidates default parameter values in the `$_default` property into the specified `$config` array. Any parameters specified in the original `$config` array will take precedence over corresponding parameters specified in `$_default`.

- `parseFile()` and `parseString()` pass the modified `$config` parameter with all other provided parameters to their respective methods in the `tidy` class and return the resulting return values.

Options

Tidy includes a lot of configuration options, but a small number of them are relevant in the context of this book.

Two options deal with output formats applicable for web scraping: `'output-html'` and `'output-xhtml'`; both take Boolean values. These options are mutually exclusive, meaning you can set one to `true` at any given time. Generally, `'output-xhtml'` is preferable, as it's stricter and produces more predictable output, but it may not be usable in some cases. It's crucial to compare Tidy output to the original document to confirm that correction of document malformations hasn't resulted in data loss. Comparing the lengths of the original and modified documents to ensure their ratio isn't beyond a certain threshold can provide a reasonable sanity check.

Document encoding is one area where issues may arise later depending on the configuration of Tidy when it's used. For example, the XMLReader extension uses UTF-8 encoding internally, which may be problematic if your input document does not. `'input-encoding'` and `'output-encoding'` control the assumed encoding for each. See the Tidy documentation for either of these settings or the documentation for the `$config` parameter of the `parseFile()` and `parseString()` methods for more information on supported encodings.

Other options are useful mainly for debugging purposes and you should generally turn them off in production environments. This is a good reason for subclassing the `tidy` class to control default option values, so that two separate sets are accessible for different development environments.

Three of these options are `'indent'`, `'indent-spaces'`, and `'indent-attributes'`. The first of these, `'indent'`, takes a Boolean value indicating whether Tidy should apply indentation to make the hierarchical relationships between elements more visually prominent. `'indent-spaces'` takes an integer containing the number of whitespace characters used to denote a single level of indentation, defaulting to 2. Lastly, `'indent-attributes'` takes a boolean value indicating whether each attribute within an element should begin on a new line.

Speaking of attributes, `'sort-attributes'` can take the string `'alpha'` to have element attributes sorted alphabetically. It's set to `'none'` by default, which disables sorting.

If lines within a document tend to be long and difficult to read, the `'wrap'` option may be useful. It takes an integer representing the number of characters per line that Tidy should allow before forcing a new line. It's set to 68 by default and you can disable it entirely by setting it to 0.

---

[5]   `array_merge()`: *http://php.net/array_merge*

Having no empty lines to separate blocks can also make markup challenging to read. `'vertical-space'` takes a Boolean value intended to help with this by adding empty lines for readability. It's disabled by default.

Debugging

As good a job as it does, Tidy may not always be able to clean documents. When using Tidy to repair a document, it's generally a good idea to check for what issues it encounters.

Tidy has two types of issues to check for when using it for web scraping analysis: warnings and errors. Like their PHP counterparts, warnings are non-fatal and generally have some sort of automated response that Tidy executes to handle them. Errors are not necessarily fatal but Tidy may have no way to handle them.

An error buffer stores all issues regardless of their type. Accessing information in and about this buffer is one area in which the procedural and object-oriented APIs for the Tidy extension differ.

```
// Procedural
$issues = tidy_get_error_buffer($tidy);

// Object-oriented
$issues = $tidy->errorBuffer;
```

Note that `errorBuffer` is a property of the `$tidy` object, not a method. Also note the slight difference in naming conventions between the procedural function and the object property, versus the consistency held throughout most other areas of the APIs.

The error buffer is not useful in string form. Below is a code sample derived from a user-contributed comment on the PHP manual page for `tidy_get_error_buffer()`[6]. This code parses individual components of each issue into arrays where they are more accessible.

Listing 9.3

```
 1. <?php
 2. preg_match_all(
 3.     '/^(?:line (?P<line>\d+) column (?P<column>\d+) - )?' .
 4.     '(?P<type>\S+): (?:\[(?:\d+\.?){4}]:)?(?P<message>.*)?$/m',
 5.     $tidy->errorBuffer, // or tidy_get_error_buffer($tidy)
 6.     $issues,
 7.     PREG_SET_ORDER
 8. );
 9.
10. print_r($issues);
```

---

[6]   `tidy_get_error_buffer()`: *https://php.net/tidy.props.errorbuffer*

Example output:

```
Array
(
    [0] => Array
        (
            [0] => line 12 column 1 - Warning: <meta> element not
                empty or not closed
            [line] => 12
            [1] => 12
            [column] => 1
            [2] => 1
            [type] => Warning
            [3] => Warning
            [message] => <meta> element not empty or not closed
            [4] => <meta> element not empty or not closed
        )
)
```

The Tidy extension also provides a way to get at the number of warnings and errors encountered without requiring that you manually parse the error buffer. The procedural API supports this feature, but the object-oriented API does not.

```
$warnings = tidy_warning_count($tidy);
$errors = tidy_error_count($tidy);
```

You can add this feature to the object-oriented API by subclassing the tidy class.

Listing 9.4

```
 1. <?php
 2. class mytidy extends tidy
 3. {
 4.     public function warningCount() {
 5.         return tidy_warning_count($this);
 6.     }
 7.
 8.     public function errorCount() {
 9.         return tidy_error_count($this);
10.     }
11. }
```

Output

Obtaining the resulting output of Tidy repairing a document is simple. The procedural format is:

```
$output = tidy_get_output($tidy);
```

9. Tidy Extension

While the object-oriented API offers no public declaration of the magic method __toString(), you can typecast a Tidy instance to a string as well as output directly using the echo construct. If you've already subclassed the tidy class to get warning and error counts, you can add __toString() there too.

```
$output = (string) $tidy;
```

At this point, you should have your obtained document in a format suitable for input to an XML extension.

Chapter

10

DOM Extension

Once you've cleaned up the retrieved markup document and it validates, the next step is extracting useful data from it. For this, the ideal approach is to take advantage of the fact that the document is valid markup and use an XML extension to work with it. The next three chapters cover those offered by PHP.

The namesake of this chapter is the Document Object Model[1] (DOM) extension. This extension gets its name from a standardized language-independent API for navigating and manipulating valid and well-formed XML[2] and HTML documents. W3C, an organization devoted to emerging internet-related standards, maintains this standard. This chapter limits its scope to parts of the DOM extension that are relevant and essential to web scraping; you should not consider it a comprehensive reference.

---

[1]   Document Object Model: _http://php.net/dom_
[2]   XML: _https://phpa.me/wikibooks-xml-mde_

> **DOM XML**
>
> *The DOM extension is available in PHP 5 and PHP 7. Its PHP 4-compatible predecessor, the DOM XML extension, has a somewhat different API but the same concepts. This chapter restricts its examples to the DOM extension. Consult the related section of the PHP manual for specifics on the DOM XML extension[3].*

Types of Parsers

Before going much further, you should be aware there are two types of XML parsers: **tree parsers** and **pull parsers**. Tree parsers load the entire document into memory and allow you to access any part of it at any time as well as manipulate it. Pull parsers read the document a piece at a time and limit you to working with the last piece they read.

The two types of parsers share a relationship akin to that of `file_get_contents()` and `fgets()`. The former lets you work with the entire document at once and uses as much memory needed to store it, while the latter allows you to work with a piece of the document at a time and uses less memory in the process.

When working with reasonably large documents, minimizing memory usage should be a goal. Attempting to load a massive document into memory all at once has the potential to cause either memory usage to exceed the limit imposed by the PHP `memory_limit` setting or execution time to exceed the limit imposed by the PHP `max_execution_time` setting.

The DOM extension is a tree parser. In general, web scraping does not require the ability to access all parts of the document simultaneously. Data extraction involved in web scraping can be rather extensive to write using a pull parser. The appropriateness of one extension over the other depends on the size and complexity of the document.

Loading Documents

The `DOMDocument` class is where the use of the DOM extension begins. The first thing to do is instantiate it and then feed it the validated markup data. Note that the DOM extension emits warnings loading a document if that document is not valid or well-formed. To avoid this, see the previous chapter on using the Tidy extension. If Tidy does not address an issue, you can control error emission, as shown in the examples below. Errors persist in a buffer until manually cleared, so make a point of clearing them after each load operation if they are not needed to avoid wasting memory.

You can buffer DOM errors rather than emitting them as warnings.

```
$oldSetting = libxml_use_internal_errors(true);
```

First, instantiate a container for the document.

```
$doc = new DOMDocument;
```

---

[3]   *DOM XML extension: http://php.net/book.domxml*

You can load markup already contained within a string.

```
$doc->loadHTML($htmlString);
```

You can also load markup saved to an external file.

```
$doc->loadHTMLFile($htmlFilePath);
```

Call `libxml_get_errors` to get all errors if needed.

```
$errors = libxml_get_errors();
```

You can also get the last error.

```
$error = libxml_get_last_error();
```

This function clears any existing errors from previous operations.

```
libxml_clear_errors();
```

You can then revert error buffering to its previous setting.

```
libxml_use_internal_errors($oldSetting);
```

Tree Terminology

Once you have loaded a document, the next natural step is to extract desired data from it. Doing so requires a bit more knowledge about the structure of the DOM. Recall the earlier mention of tree parsers. If you have any computer science background, you should be glad to know the term "tree" in the context of tree parsers does refer to the data structure by the same name. If not, here is a brief run-down of related concepts.

A **tree** is a hierarchical structure (think family tree) composed of **nodes**, which exist in the DOM extension as the DOMNode class. Nodes are to trees what elements are to arrays: items existing within the data structure.

Each node can have zero or more **child nodes** which are collectively represented by a childNodes property in the DOMNode class. childNodes is an instance of the class DOMNodeList, which is precisely what it sounds like. Other related properties include firstChild and lastChild, both of which point to a DOMNode instance. **Leaf nodes** are nodes with no children, which you can check using the hasChildNodes() method of DOMNode.

All nodes in a tree have a single **parent node**, with one exception: the **root node** from which all other nodes in the tree stem. If two nodes share the same parent, they are appropriately referred to as **sibling nodes**. The previousSibling and nextSibling properties in DOMNode represent this relationship.

Lastly, child nodes of a node, child nodes of those child nodes, and so on are collectively known as **descendant nodes**. Likewise, the parent node of a node, that parent node's parent node, and so on are collectively known as **ancestor nodes**.

An example may help to showcase this terminology.

```
<html>
    <body>
        <ul id="thelist">
            <li>Foo</li>
            <li>Bar</li>
        </ul>
    </body>
</html>
```

- html is the root node.
- body is the first child of html.
- ul is the first child of body.
- The li nodes containing Foo and Bar are the first and last child nodes of ul respectively.
- The li node containing Bar node is the next sibling of the li node containing Foo.
- The li node containing Foo is likewise the previous sibling of the li node containing Bar.
- The ul and li nodes are descendants of the body node.
- The ul, body, and html nodes are likewise ancestors of the li nodes.

Elements and Attributes

At this point, the DOM transcends the tree analogy. There's more than one variety of node, or to phrase that within the context of the DOM extension, DOMNode has subclasses. The main two you'll be dealing with are DOMElement for **elements** and DOMAttr for **attributes**. Here are how these concepts apply to the example in the last section.

- ul is the name of an element.
- id is the name of an attribute of the ul element.
- thelist is the value of the id attribute.
- Foo and Bar are the values of the li elements.

Locating Nodes

Two methods of the DOMDocument class allow you to reduce the number of nodes you have to traverse to find the data you want.

getElementById()[4] attempts to locate a single element that meets two criteria: 1) it's a descendant of the document's root element; 2) it has a given id attribute value. If it finds such an element, it returns that element as a DOMElement instance; if not, it returns null.

getElementsByTagName()[5] attempts to locate all elements that meet two criteria: 1) it's a descendant of the document's root element; 2) it has a given element name (such as ul). This method always returns a DOMNodeList of any found elements. The DOMNodeList[6] class has a length property that is equal to 0 if the method finds no elements. DOMNodeList is also iterable, and you can use it as the subject of a foreach loop.

The DOMElement[7] class also has a getElementsByTagName() method, which functions the same way with the exception that located elements are descendants of that element instead of the document's root element.

Listing 10.1

```php
1.  <?php
2.  // One way get the list items in the last example
3.  $listItems = $doc->getElementsByTagName('li');
4.
5.  // A slightly more specific way (better if there are multiple lists)
6.  if ($list = $doc->getElementById('thelist')) {
7.      $listItems = $list->getElementsByTagName('li');
8.  }
9.
10. // Yet another way if the list doesn't have an id
11. $lists = $doc->getElementsByTagName('ul');
12. if ($lists->length) {
13.     $list = $lists->item(0);
14.     $listItems = $list->getElementsByTagName('li');
15. }
16.
17. // Outputs "thelist" (without quotes)
18. echo $list->getAttribute('id');
19.
20. // Outputs "Foo" on one line, then "Bar" on another
21. foreach ($listItems as $listItem) {
22.     echo $listItem->nodeValue, PHP_EOL;
23. }
24.
25. // Outputs text content inside <ul id="thelist"> and </ul>
26. echo $list->nodeValue;
```

---

[4] getElementById(): *https://php.net/domdocument.getelementbyid*
[5] getElementsByTagName(): *https://php.net/domdocument.getelementsbytagname*
[6] DOMNodeList: *https://php.net/class.domnodelist*
[7] DOMElement: *https://php.net/class.domelement*

XPath and DOMXPath

As regular expressions allow you to find instances of character patterns within strings, XPath[8] allows you to find instances of node patterns within XML-compatible documents. Both technologies fulfill their purpose by providing a syntax comprised of **meta-characters** to express these patterns concisely and succinctly. With the DOM extension, the DOMXPath class supports version 1.0 of the XPath standard.

The DOMXPath constructor has a single required parameter: an existing DOMDocument instance on which it performs queries. DOMXPath has two other relevant methods: evaluate() and query(). Both accept a string containing an XPath expression with which to query the document as their first parameter.

Optionally, you may pass a DOMNode instance associated with the document as the second parameter ($contextNode) for either method. When specified, that node becomes the **context node** and DOMXPath restricts query results to that node and its descendants. Otherwise, it assumes the root element of the document to be the context node.

The difference between evaluate() and query() is the latter always returns an instance of DOMNodeList whereas the former attempts to return an appropriately typed result if it finds one result (e.g., a string for an attribute value).

Absolute Addressing

Addressing is the act of using an XPath expression to get a set of nodes to which that expression applies. The rest of this chapter covers aspects of addressing and related expression syntax.

XPath expressions share similarities with UNIX filesystem paths; both traverse conceptual tree structures. See the example below for specific instances of this. The previous HTML example used to illustrate concepts of markup languages showcases XPath addressing in this example.

Listing 10.2

```php
1. <?php
2. // Load a markup document
3. $doc = new DOMDocument;
4. $doc->loadHTML('
5.    <html>
6.    <body>
7.    <ul id="thelist">
8.       <li>Foo</li>
9.       <li>Bar</li>
10.   </ul>
11.   </body>
12.   </html>
13. ');
```

---

[8]   XPath: http://schlitt.info/opensource/blog/0704_xpath.html

```
14.
15. // Configure an object to query the document
16. $xpath = new DOMXPath($doc);
17.
18. // Returns a DOMNodeList with only the html node
19. $list = $xpath->query('/html');
20.
21. // Returns a DOMNodeList with only the body node
22. $list = $xpath->query('/html/body');
23.
24. // Also returns a DOMNodeList with only the body node
25. $list = $xpath->query('//body');
```

- In the first two examples, the expression references the root element (html) even though it assumes that element to be the context node (since neither query() call receives a node as its second parameter).
- A **single forward slash** / indicates a parent-child relationship. /html/body addresses all body nodes that are children of the document's root html element (which in this case amounts to a single result).
- A **double forward slash** // indicates an ancestor-descendant relationship. //body addresses all body nodes that are descendants of the context node (which again amounts to a single result).

You can use the single and double forward slash operators more than once and in combination with each other as shown below.

The following returns all ul nodes that are descendants of the body node

```
$list = $xpath->query('//body//ul');
```

This query returns all li nodes that are children of the ul nodes.

```
$list = $xpath->query('//body//ul/li');
```

Namespaces

If you attempt to address nodes by their element name and receive no results when it appears you should, it's possible, albeit unlikely, the document is namespacing nodes. The easiest way to get around this is to replace the element name with a condition.

For example, if you are using the expression //ul, an expression that disregards the namespace would be //*[name()="ul"] where * is a wildcard for all nodes and the name() function compares the node name against a given value.

Relative Addressing

The above examples use **absolute addressing**, similar in concept to absolute filesystem paths. The next example covers using **relative addressing**. It returns all ul nodes that have li child nodes.

```
$list = $xpath->query('//body//ul/li/..');
```

Where //body//ul/li selects li nodes, //body//ul/li/.. instead selects ul nodes by using relative addressing (specifically ..) to request the parent node of the addressed node (li) rather than the addressed node itself. Compare this with the same sequence used to refer to the parent directory of the current directory on a UNIX filesystem.

Addressing Attributes

Examples thus far have dealt with element nodes in particular. XPath also supports the selection of attribute nodes.

This query returns the id attribute of all ul nodes.

```
$list = $xpath->query('//ul/@id');
```

The following XPath query returns all ul nodes that have id attributes.

```
$list = $xpath->query('//ul/@id/..');
```

This query returns all id attribute nodes.

```
$list = $xpath->query('//@id');
```

- //ul/@id addresses all id attribute nodes associated with ul element nodes that are descendants of the context node.
- Note how the use of relative addressing in the second example applies to attributes nodes as it would apply to child element nodes.
- //@id addresses all id attribute nodes that are descendants of the context node regardless of their associated element.

Unions

When addressing nodes, it's possible to perform a single query with more than one expression. Such a query addresses the **union** of those expressions.

The first example returns all list items (li) of both unordered (ul) and ordered (ol) lists.

```
$list = $xpath->query('//ol/li|//ul/li');
```

The second example returns all header (th) and data (td) cells of table rows (tr).

```
$list = $xpath->query('//tr/th|//tr/td');
```

Conditions

Like addressing nodes based on their surrounding hierarchical structure, you can also address them based on **conditions**.

Square brackets delimit a conditional expression. This query returns all ul nodes with an id attribute node.

```
$list = $xpath->query('//ul[@id]');
```

You can reference element and attribute nodes the same way within a condition as you would outside of one. That is, you refer to elements by their name and prefix attribute names with @. This query returns all li child nodes of the ul node with an id of "thelist".

```
$list = $xpath->query('//ul[@id = "thelist"]/li');
```

A condition comprised of a single number is short for position() = # where # is the number used. position() is a function that returns the position of each node within the current context. You can return the first ul node that is a descendant of the context node.

```
$list = $xpath->query('//ul[1]');
```

Or you can query to return the first li child node of each ul node.

```
$list = $xpath->query('//ul/li[1]');
```

This query returns all ul nodes containing a li node with the value "foobar".

```
$list = $xpath->query('//ul[li = "foobar"]');
```

The = operator handles equality comparisons. The converse, the != operator checks for inequality. Other standard comparison operators are also supported including <, <=, >, and >=.

Using PHP Functions

As of PHP 5.3, it's possible to use functions defined in PHP within XPath expressions. You can do this using the registerPHPFunctions()[9] method of the DOMXPath class.

---

[9]   registerPHPFunctions(): *https://php.net/domxpath.registerphpfunctions*

Listing 10.3

```php
1.  <?php
2.  $doc = new DOMDocument;
3.  $xpath = new DOMXPath($doc);
4.
5.  // This allows any PHP function to be used
6.  $xpath->registerPHPFunctions();
7.
8.  // This allows only the substr() PHP function to be used
9.  $xpath->registerPHPFunctions('substr');
10.
11. // This allows only the substr() and strpos() PHP functions to be used
12. $xpath->registerPHPFunctions(['substr', 'strpos']);
13.
14. // Attempting to use a disallowed function results in a warning like this:
15. // Warning: DOMXPath::query(): Not allowed to call handler 'strtolower()'
```

You can use PHP functions within XPath expressions in two ways.

The first is useful for extracting and performing operations on string values contained within nodes or attributes.

```php
$nodes = $xpath->query('//ul[php:functionString("substr", li, 0, 3) = "foo"]');
```

To use a PHP function here, invoke the php:functionString() function within the XPath expression. The first argument to this function is a string containing the name of the PHP function to invoke, in this case "substr". All other arguments are passed to the PHP function invoked.

In the above example, where the first parameter $string passed to the substr()[10] PHP function would typically be a string literal or a variable containing a string value, li indicates a node with that name. You can also use attributes, prefixed with an @ symbol as normal.

The second and third parameters of substr(), $start and $length, receive the values 0 and 3 respectively.

Ergo, the above example locates ul nodes containing li nodes where the first three characters of the li node value are equal to the string "foo".

The second method of invoking PHP functions in XPath expressions deals with an array of node objects.

```php
function multiple($nodes) {
    return count($nodes) > 1;
}

$nodes = $xpath->query('//ul[php:function("multiple", li)]');
```

---

[10] substr(): http://php.net/substr

This example uses the user-defined function `multiple()` by invoking `php:function()` within the XPath expression. Like `php:functionString()`, `php:function()` takes the name of the PHP function to invoke as its first argument and any arguments to pass to that PHP function as its later arguments.

The difference in behavior between the two is, rather than receiving a string value, the PHP function invoked receives an array of node instances of appropriate classes (e.g., `DOMElement`, `DOMAttr`, etc.).

In this example, the return value of the `multiple()` function is a Boolean value that XPath uses to filter the nodes returned by `query()`. More specifically, this example locates `ul` nodes containing more than one `li` node as designated by the `multiple()` function.

Resources

This chapter covers a fraction of what XPath offers, mainly basic concepts and areas applicable when using XPath to extract data from retrieved markup documents. You can find other functions, operators, and more advanced concepts detailed further in the resources cited below. Review of those resources is highly recommended for more extensive and complex data extraction applications.

1. DOM Level 3 Core standard[11]
2. DOM Level 3 XPath standard[12]

---

[11] DOM Level 3 Core standard: http://www.w3.org/TR/DOM-Level-3-Core
[12] DOM Level 3 XPath standard: http://www.w3.org/TR/DOM-Level-3-XPath

Chapter

11

SimpleXML Extension

Like the DOM extension, the SimpleXML extension[1] provides a tree parser. The DOM extension keeps an API consistent with that of the standard on which it's based. The API offered by SimpleXML is one most PHP developers should find to be less massive, more intuitive, and easier to use compared to the DOM extension.

SimpleXML makes use of the flexibility and versatility of PHP arrays by using them to access both individual elements from a collection with the same element name as well as element attributes. It also adds iterability to markup documents, making them simple to traverse.

These advantages do not come without cost. Like other tree parsers, SimpleXML must parse the entire document before you can use it. As such, it tends to be slower when parsing larger documents than a pull parser like *XMLReader*. For a script dealing with a smaller document, however, SimpleXML works well.

---

[1]   SimpleXML extension: *http://php.net/book.simplexml*

Loading a Document

Where DOMDocument is the central class in the DOM extension, SimpleXMLElement is its counterpart in the SimpleXML extension. Loading a markup document is as simple as specifying it via the class constructor.

The following constructor invocation loads markup already contained within a string when instantiating SimpleXMLElement.

```php
$sxe = new SimpleXMLElement($markupString);
```

The constructor's second parameter (specified as null in the second example shown below) allows for further configuration of the instance. For documents with less than valid markup, using the value LIBXML_NOERROR | LIBXML_NOWARNING for this parameter may be useful as it suppresses error and warning reports.

The third parameter used in the second constructor call receives a value of true which indicates that $filePath is a path to a file or URL containing markup rather than the markup itself.

```php
$sxe = new SimpleXMLElement($filePath, null, true);
```

Accessing Elements

Use of SimpleXML looks a bit like XPath expressions, except the API accomplishes the same effect as formatted expressions stored in strings. Unlike XPath expressions, SimpleXML automatically assumes that element access is relative to the root node.

Listing 11.1

```php
1.  <?php
2.  $markupString = '
3.      <html>
4.      <body>
5.      <ul id="thelist">
6.          <li>Foo</li>
7.          <li>Bar</li>
8.      </ul>
9.      </body>
10.     </html>
11. ';
12.
13. // Outputs "Foo" -- note that the "html" element isn't referenced
14. $sxe = new SimpleXMLElement($markupString);
15. echo $sxe->body->ul->li[0];
16.
17. // Also works, assumes the first "li" element if several are present
18. echo $sxe->body->ul->li;
19.
```

```
20. // Outputs "ul"
21. echo $sxe->body->ul->getName(), PHP_EOL;
22.
23. // Outputs "Foo" then "Bar"
24. foreach ($sxe->body->ul->li as $li) {
25.     echo $li, PHP_EOL;
26. }
27.
28. // Does the same thing
29. foreach ($sxe->body->ul->children() as $li) {
30.     echo $li, PHP_EOL;
31. }
```

When referencing a child element of the current element (via the body property of $sxe above, for example), the accessed child element is also an instance of SimpleXMLElement. It's possible to chain element access and to reference the last element in such a chain using a variable. See the first foreach loop shown above for an example of both of these.

Accessing Attributes

Where element access makes use of enumerated arrays for accessing elements with the same name on the same hierarchical level, attribute access makes use of associative arrays. The example below uses the same $markupString sample data as in the previous example.

Given the markup in Listing 11, you can access attributes directly by their names.

```
// Outputs "thelist"
echo $sxe->body->ul['id'];
```

You can also use the attributes method available on an element to access all attributes without having to know their names.

```
// Outputs "id=thelist"
foreach ($sxe->body->ul->attributes() as $name => $value) {
    echo $name, '=', $value, PHP_EOL;
}
```

If you do know an attribute name, you can access it directly after calling attributes().

```
// Another way to output "thelist"
$attrs = $sxe->body->ul->attributes();
echo $attrs->id;
```

What the attributes() method returns is a SimpleXMLElement instance which provides access to attribute names and values in the same way SimpleXMLElement makes child elements and their values available. As such, you can use the returned instance as the subject of a foreach loop to iterate over the properties it exposes.

```
<!-- Actual markup -->
<ul id="thelist"></ul>

<!-- How attributes() exposes it as a SimpleXMLElement instance -->
<ul>
    <id>thelist</id>
</ul>
```

A Debugging Bug

Bug #44973[2], which affects the SimpleXML extension, is reportedly present in PHP 5.2.6 and may be present in other versions as well. To expose the bug, attempt to output a node accessed via a SimpleXMLElement instance using echo, print_r(), var_dump(), *and other similar functions. If the node has both attributes and a text value, the output of these functions does not show the attributes. This does not mean that attribute values are not accessible in this situation; they can't be output in this fashion unless referenced directly. The status of this ticket is "not a bug" at the time of this writing, but comments on the ticket provide workarounds.*

Comparing Nodes

To compare an element or attribute with a string value, you must first explicitly cast it to a string. Otherwise, it is treated as an object, which may cause type issues, including emitting errors.

```
if ((string) $sxe->body->ul['id'] == 'thelist') {
    echo htmlentities((string) $sxe->body->ul['id']);
}
```

DOM Interoperability

With both the DOM and SimpleXML extensions being tree parsers, this allows for a certain degree of interoperability between the two. This can be handy if you prefer one over the other when refactoring legacy code or if you have use cases for both within a single application.

This function converts a SimpleXMLElement to a DOMElement.

```
$domElement = dom_import_simplexml($simpleXmlElement);
```

This function converts a DOMNode to a SimpleXMLElement.

```
$simpleXmlElement = simplexml_import_dom($domNode);
```

---

[2]   Bug #44973: http://bugs.php.net/bug.php?id=44973

XPath

Like the DOM extension, SimpleXML also supports XPath. Rather than using a separate class for it as the DOM does, the SimpleXMLElement class itself includes a method for it. Where the query() and evaluate() methods of the DOMXPath class return a DOMNodeList instance, the xpath() method of SimpleXMLElement instead returns an enumerated array of SimpleXMLElement instances that match the given XPath expression.

```php
// Returns all list items from the previous example
$elements = $sxe->xpath('//ul[@id="thelist"]/li');

// Outputs "Foo" then "Bar"
foreach ($elements as $li) {
    echo $li, PHP_EOL;
}
```

This chapter should give you a good idea of how the SimpleXML extension functions and the ease of use it provides. It's short because, beyond a certain point, the SimpleXML extension is best learned by experimentation with real-world data rather than by example.

In general, SimpleXML is a better choice for simpler documents, as it requires writing less code in such instances. It's also the easier to understand option when you're just beginning to learn how to process XML. Eventually, you develop a feel for when to use SimpleXML and when DOM should be the preferred solution.

Chapter

12

XMLReader Extension

The previous two chapters have covered two available XML extensions that use tree parsers. This chapter focuses on the XMLReader extension[1], which implements a pull parser.

As mentioned in the chapter on the _DOM extension_, pull parsers differ from tree parsers in that they read documents in a piecewise fashion rather than loading them into memory all at once. A consequence of this is pull parsers generally traverse documents once in one direction and leave you to collect whatever data is relevant to you along the way.

Before getting started, a noteworthy point is XMLReader's underlying library, libxml, uses UTF-8 encoding internally. As such, you can mitigate encoding issues if you encode any document you import (e.g., one you've cleaned using the Tidy extension) appropriately to avoid issues with different encodings.

---

[1]   XMLReader extension: _http://www.php.net/book.xmlreader_

> **XML Parser**
>
> *The XML Parser extension[2], as the PHP manual refers to it, is a predecessor of XMLReader from the days of PHP 4 and is not actively maintained. Its API focuses on a more event-driven style of programming as opposed to the iterative orientation of the XMLReader extension.*

Loading a Document

The focal class of the XMLReader extension is aptly named XMLReader. It doesn't declare a constructor, but instead offers two methods for feeding XML data into it.

The static xml()[3] method loads a document contained within a string.

```
$doc = XMLReader::xml($xmlString);
```

To load a document from an external file, use the static open()[4] method.

```
$doc = XMLReader::open($filePath);
```

Both of these methods have two more parameters.

The second parameter is a string specifying the encoding scheme for the input document. It's optional and defaults to 'UTF-8' if unspecified or specified as null. Valid values for this parameter aren't included in the PHP manual but you can find them in the reference for the underlying libxml2 library[5].

The third parameter is an integer value you can set in bitmask fashion using constants[6] from the libxml extension. This parameter is the preferred method to configure the parser over using the deprecated setParserProperty() method. The table below lists the specific constants that you can use to form the bitmask (using the bitwise OR operator |).

Contact	Description
LIBXML_COMPACT	Activate optimization of small nodes allocation. May speed up application.
LIBXML_DTDATTR	Default DTD attributes.
LIBXML_DTDLOAD	Load the external subset.
LIBXML_DTDVALID	Validate with the DTD.
LIBXML_NOBLANKS	Remove blank nodes.
LIBXML_NOCDATA	Merge CDATA as text nodes.

---

[2]   XML Parser extension: *http://php.net/book.xml*
[3]   xml(): *https://php.net/xmlreader.xml*
[4]   open(): *https://php.net/xmlreader.open*
[5]   libxml2 library: *http://www.xmlsoft.org/encoding.html#Default*
[6]   constants: *http://php.net/libxml.constants*

Contact	Description
LIBXML_NOENT	Substitute entities.
LIBXML_NOERROR	Suppress error reports.
LIBXML_NONET	Disable network access when loading documents.
LIBXML_NOWARNING	Suppress warning reports.
LIBXML_NSCLEAN	Remove redundant namespace declarations.
LIBXML_XINCLUDE	Implement XInclude substitution.

As an example, a call that configured the parser to suppress errors and warnings looks like the following.

```
$doc = XMLReader::xml($xmlString, null, LIBXML_NOERROR | LIBXML_NOWARNING);
```

Iteration

The XMLReader instance acts as both an iterator over the entire document and a data object for the current node pointed to by that iterator. It contains a set of properties[7] which represent those of the current node. It updates these properties as the iterator position changes.

```
while ($doc->read()) {
    // ...
}
```

The read() method attempts to move the iterator position to the next node and returns a Boolean value indicating if it succeeded or failed. That is, it returns false once it reaches the end of the document. As such, it's perfect for use in a while loop, as shown above.

Nodes

As in other extensions, each node has a type stored in the reader's nodeType property. The types you are generally interested in are still elements (XMLReader::ELEMENT) and attributes (XMLReader::ATTRIBUTE), possibly also text (XMLReader::TEXT) and CDATA (XMLReader::CDATA) elements as well. The XMLReader extension also has a node type for ending elements (i.e., closing tags), XMLReader::END_ELEMENT. Its importance should become more obvious in the next section.

---

[7]   properties: https://phpa.me/xmlreader-props

The example below shows how to check the node type against an appropriate constant[8].

```php
while ($doc->read()) {
    if ($doc->nodeType == XMLReader::ELEMENT) {
        var_dump($doc->localName);
        var_dump($doc->value);
        var_dump($doc->hasValue);
    }
}
```

Also, like other extensions, nodes have names. Two properties represent these: name and localName. The former represents the fully qualified name, including the namespace specification, while the latter represents the node name by itself and is the one you generally want to use.

Elements and Attributes

Attribute nodes can have values. When the iterator points to an attribute node, it populates the value property with the node's value. You can use the hasValue property to check for its presence.

Element nodes can have attributes. When the iterator points to an element node, the hasAttributes property indicates the presence of attributes and you can use the getAttribute() method to get an attribute value in the form of a string.

Here is an HTML table you might want to parse.

Listing 12.1

```html
 1. <table id="thetable">
 2.     <tr>
 3.         <td>row 0 col 0</td>
 4.         <td>row 0 col 1</td>
 5.     </tr>
 6.     <tr>
 7.         <td>row 1 col 0</td>
 8.         <td>row 1 col 1</td>
 9.     </tr>
10. </table>
```

The example in Listing 12.2 uses some of these together to parse data from an HTML table.

---

[8]   appropriate constant: https://phpa.me/xmlreader-constants

Listing 12.2

```php
1.  <?php
2.  $inTable = false;
3.  $tableData = [];
4.
5.  while ($doc->read()) {
6.      switch ($doc->nodeType) {
7.          case XMLREADER::ELEMENT:
8.              if ($doc->localName == 'table'
9.                  && $doc->getAttribute('id') == 'thetable') {
10.                 $inTable = true;
11.             } elseif ($inTable && $doc->localName == 'tr') {
12.                 $row = count($tableData);
13.                 $tableData[$row] = [];
14.             } elseif ($inTable && $doc->localName == 'td') {
15.                 $tableData[$row][] = $doc->readString();
16.             }
17.             break;
18.         case XMLREADER::END_ELEMENT:
19.             if ($inTable && $doc->localName == 'table') {
20.                 $inTable = false;
21.             }
22.             break;
23.     }
24. }
25.
26. var_export($tableData);
```

Results in the following output.

```
array (
  0 =>
  array (
    0 => 'row 0 col 0',
    1 => 'row 0 col 1',
  ),
  1 =>
  array (
    0 => 'row 1 col 0',
    1 => 'row 1 col 1',
  ),
)
```

This example showcases the main difference between pull parsers and tree parsers: pull parsers have no concept of hierarchical context. They are aware of the node to which the iterator points; that's all. As such, you must create your indicators of context where you need them.

This example checks the node type as it reads nodes. It ignores any node that isn't either an opening or closing element. If it encounters an opening element, it evaluates the element name ($doc->localName) to confirm it's a table and examines the element's id attribute value ($doc->getAttribute('id')) to confirm it has a value of 'thetable'. If so, it sets a flag variable $inTable to true. This variable indicates to later if branch conditions that the iterator points to a node within the desired table.

It enters the next if branch when it encounters the table row elements within the table. A combination of checking the node name and the $inTable flag facilitates this. When it enters the branch, it initializes a new element in the $tableData array to an empty array. This array later stores data from cells in that row. It stores the key associated with the row in $tableData in the $row variable.

When it encounters table cell elements, it executes the last if branch. Like the row branch, this branch checks the node name and the $inTable flag. If the check passes, it then stores the current node's value in the array associated with the current table row using the readString() method.

Here's where the XMLREADER::END_ELEMENT node type comes into play. Once the example reaches the end of the table, it shouldn't read any further data into the array. If the ending element has the name 'table' and the $inTable flag indicates the iterator points to a node within the desired table, the flag is then set to false. Since no other tables should theoretically have the same ID attribute, no if branches execute in later while loop iterations.

If this was the one table of interest in the document, it would be prudent to replace the $inTable = false; statement with a break 2; statement. Doing so terminates the while loop used to read nodes from the document as soon as it encounters the end of the table, preventing any further unnecessary read operations.

readString() Availability

As its entry in the PHP manual notes, the presence of the readString()[9] method used in the above example depends on the version of the underlying libxml library used by the XMLReader extension. If this method is unavailable in your environment, Listing 12.3 shows an alternative approach for getting the node value.

---

[9]   readString(): *https://php.net/xmlreader.readstring*

Listing 12.3

```php
1.  <?php
2.  $inTable = false;
3.  $inCell = false;
4.  $tableData = [];
5.
6.  while ($doc->read()) {
7.      switch ($doc->nodeType) {
8.          case XMLREADER::ELEMENT:
9.              if ($doc->localName == 'table' && $doc->getAttribute('id') == 'thetable') {
10.                 $inTable = true;
11.             } elseif ($inTable && $doc->localName == 'tr') {
12.                 $row = count($tableData);
13.                 $tableData[$row] = [];
14.             } elseif ($inTable && $doc->localName == 'td') {
15.                 $cell = count($tableData[$row]);
16.                 $tableData[$row][$cell] = '';
17.                 $inCell = true;
18.             }
19.             break;
20.
21.         case XMLREADER::END_ELEMENT:
22.             if ($inTable && $doc->localName == 'table') {
23.                 $inTable = false;
24.             } elseif ($inCell && $doc->localName == 'td') {
25.                 $inCell = false;
26.             }
27.             break;
28.
29.         case XMLREADER::TEXT:
30.         case XMLREADER::CDATA:
31.             if ($inCell) {
32.                 $tableData[$row][$cell] .= $doc->value;
33.             }
34.             break;
35.     }
36. }
```

This modified example adds opening and closing table cell checks that toggle their own flag $inCell and switch cases for the TEXT and CDATA node types that check $inCell and, when it's set to true, add the contents of the value property from the XMLReader instance to the $tableData array.

DOM Interoperation

One nice feature of the XMLReader extension is the expand() method, which returns an object of the DOM extension class for the node pointed to by the iterator. Element nodes, for example, cause this method to return a DOMElement instance.

The example below illustrates a modification to the previous example and provides another alternative to the readString() method for getting at the contents of table cells by taking advantage of this DOM interoperability.

```
if ($doc->localName == 'td' && $inTable) {
    $node = $doc->expand();
    $tableData[$row][] = $node->nodeValue;
}
```

Closing Documents

After conducting all necessary read operations on a document, you should call the close() method of the XMLReader instance to cleanly end file access or otherwise show you no longer need access to the original data source.

Chapter

13

CSS Selector Libraries

This chapter reviews libraries built on top of the XML extensions described in previous chapters. These libraries provide interfaces that use CSS selector expressions to query markup documents rather than a programmatic API or XPath expressions. If you are unfamiliar with CSS selectors, this chapter showcases basic expressions alongside their XPath equivalents.

> **CSS Versions**
>
> *The CSS standard has more than one version and supported selectors vary with each version. This chapter covers a subset of the selectors available in CSS3 and notes which libraries support particular CSS standard versions where available. See w3.org for a list of differences[1] between the two common versions, CSS2 and CSS3.*

---

[1]   list of differences: https://phpa.me/css-selectors-3

Reason to Use Them

Before getting into the "how" of using CSS selector libraries, it's probably best to get the "why" (and "why not") out of the way first. These libraries add a layer of complexity to applications using them, introducing another potential point of failure. They are expression parsers that take CSS selector expressions as their input and translate them into userland operations, which can have an impact on performance.

Those points aside, they do offer a syntax that may be more intuitive than XPath. Most developers these days know at least some CSS and probably have a little experience with a JavaScript library that uses CSS selectors for node selection on the client side, such as jQuery. Thus, knowledge of that particular area is transferable to the server side when you use libraries based on it.

To sum this up, if you're concerned about performance or simplicity of the application insofar as the number of components on which it's dependent, it's best to stick with XPath. Otherwise, CSS selector libraries are worthy of consideration for making use of a common, existing skill set.

Even if you decide to stick with XPath, keep reading. This chapter also shows XPath equivalents for each set of explained CSS selectors, which may help to further your understanding of XPath. These comparisons are not necessarily comprehensive, and there may be more than one way to express the same thing in any given case.

> **jQuery Examples**
>
> *The documentation for the jQuery library itself has visual client-side examples of selectors. If you find you aren't certain you understand any of the descriptions of CSS selectors[2] that follow, the jQuery demos and source code may be helpful supplements.*

Basics

Let's look at some basic selectors and their results when applied to a markup example.

Listing 13.1

```
1.  <html>
2.  <body>
3.  <div id="nav">
4.      <ul class="horizontal">
5.          <li><a href="/home">Home</a></li>
6.          <li><a href="/about-us">About Us</a></li>
7.          <li><a href="/contact-us">Contact Us</a></li>
8.      </ul>
9.      <img src="/img/ad1.jpg" alt="Advertisement #1">
10.     <img src="/img/ad2.jpg" alt="Advertisement #2">
11. </div>
12. </body>
13. </html>
```

---

[2]   CSS selectors: *http://api.jquery.com/category/selectors/*

- #nav selects the div element because it has an id attribute value of nav.
- li selects all li elements by their node name.
- .horizontal selects the ul element because it has a class of horizontal. (Note that elements can have more than one class.)
- * selects all elements in the document.
- li, a selects all li and a elements in the document by combining the two selectors li and a into a comma-delimited list.

The table here summarizes the XPath equivalents alongside their respective CSS counterparts. Aside from the .class selector, the XPath expressions are not much longer or more complex.

Selector	CSS	XPath
id	#nav	//*[@id="nav"]
element	li	//li
class	.horizontal	//*[@class="horizontal" \ or starts-with(@class, "horizontal ") \ or contains(@class, " horizontal ") \ or ends-with(@class, " horizontal")]
wildcard	*	//*
multiple	li, a	//li|//a

Hierarchical Selectors

Let's move on to hierarchical selectors, which use document structure as a way to select elements, using the previous markup example.

- body ul selects all ul elements that are descendants of body elements.
- ul > li selects all li elements that are children of ul elements.
- ul + img selects all img elements that immediately follow a ul sibling element (i.e., are their next sibling).
- ul ~ img selects all img elements that follow a ul sibling element (i.e., come after them and have the same parent node).

The third and fourth items in this list probably look reasonably similar. The difference is in the word "immediately." In our example, the third item in the list would only select the "Advertisement #1" image because it comes immediately after its ul sibling element in the document. The fourth item in the list, on the other hand, would select both images because both follow their ul sibling element.

Selector	CSS	XPath
ancestor descendant	body ul	//body//ul
parent > child	ul > li	//ul/li
previous + next	ul + img	//ul/following-sibling::img[1]
previous ~ siblings	ul ~ img	//ul/following-sibling::img

Basic Filters

The selectors reviewed up to this point in the chapter have always changed the types of selected nodes. Conversely, when you append a filter to an expression, it merely restricts the returned set of nodes to a subset of those matching the original expression.

Note that available filters vary per library. Support for filters in jQuery is reasonably comprehensive, and as such, it's used as the primary reference for sections related to filters in this chapter.

- `li:first` selects the first `li` node found in the document.
- `li:last` likewise selects the last `li` node found in the document.
- `li:even` selects all evenly positioned nodes in the document beginning from 0.
- `li:odd` likewise selects all oddly positioned nodes in the document, also beginning from 0.
- `li:eq(0)` selects the `li` node with a position of 0 within the set of `li` nodes (i.e., the first one) in the document.
- `li:gt(0)` selects all `li` nodes with a position greater than 0 within the set of `li` nodes (i.e., all but the first one) in the document.
- `li:lt(1)` selects all `li` nodes with a position less than 1 within the set of `li` nodes (i.e., the first one) in the document.
- `:header` matches all header nodes (i.e., h1, h2, etc.)
- `:not(:first)` negates the `:first` selector and thus selects all `li` nodes except the first one in the document.

Selector	CSS	XPath
first node	li:first	//li[1]
last node	li:last	//li[last()]
even nodes	li:even	//li[position() mod 2 = 0]
odd nodes	li:odd	//li[position() mod 2 = 1]
specific node	li:eq(0)	//li[1]
all nodes after	li:gt(0)	//li[position() > 1]
all nodes before	li:lt(1)	//li[position() < 2]
header nodes	:header	//h1|//h2|//h3|//h4|//h5|//h6
all nodes not matching an expression	:not(:first)	//*[not(position() = 1)]

When reading this table, CSS selectors begin set indices at 0 whereas XPath begins them at 1.

Content Filters

Where basic filters focus on the node type or the position of a node in the result set, content filters focus on node value or surrounding hierarchical structure.

- `a:contains("About Us")` selects all `a` nodes where the node value contains the case-sensitive substring `"About Us"`.
- `img:empty` selects all `img` nodes that contain no child nodes (including text nodes).
- `li:has(a:contains("About Us"))` selects all `li` nodes that contain an `a` node with the case-sensitive substring `"About Us"` in its node value.
- `li:parent` selects all `li` nodes that contain child nodes (including text nodes).

Selector	CSS	XPath
nodes containing text	`a:contains("About Us")`	`//a[contains(text(), "About Us")]`
nodes without children	`img:empty`	`//img[not(node())]`
nodes containing a selector match	`li:has(a:contains("About Us"))`	`//li//a[contains(text(), "About Us")]`
nodes with children	`li:parent`	`//li[node()]`

Attribute Filters

Up to this point, filters have been specific to element nodes, but they also exist for attribute nodes. Square brackets surround attribute filters in both CSS and XPath, but differ in that CSS mainly uses operators for conditions while XPath mainly uses functions. Unlike other filters described in this chapter, support for attribute filters is nearly universal between different libraries.

- `[href]` matches all nodes that have an attribute node with the name `href`.
- `[href="/home"]` matches all nodes with an attribute node named `href` that has a value of `"/home"`.
- `[href!="/home"]` matches all nodes with an attribute node named `href` that do not have a value of `"/home"`.
- `[href^="/"]` matches all nodes with an attribute node named `href` and have a value that starts with `"/"`.
- `[href$="-us"]` matches all nodes with an attribute node named `href` and have a value that ends with `"-us"`.
- `[href*="-us"]` matches all nodes with an attribute node named `href` and have a value that contains `"-us"` anywhere within the value.

- [src*="ad"][alt^="Advertisement"] matches all nodes that have both an attribute node named src with a value containing "ad" and an attribute node named alt with a value starting with "Advertisement".

Selector	CSS	XPath
has attribute	[href]	//*[@href]
has attribute value	[href="/home"]	//*[@href="/home"]
has different attribute value	[href!="/home"]	//*[@href!="/home"]
has attribute value starting with substring	[href^="/"]	//*[starts-with(@href, "/")]
has attribute value ending with substring	[href$="-us"]	//*[ends-width(@href, "-us")]
has attribute value containing substring	[href*="-us"]	//*[contains(@href, "-us")]
multiple attribute filters	[src*="ad"][alt^="Advertisement"]	//*[contains(@src, "ad") and starts-with(@alt, "Advertisement")]

Child Filters

Child filters are similar to the basic filters reviewed earlier, except applied to child nodes.

- ul:nth-child(2) selects the second child element within each ul node. The parameter passed to the filter can also be even or odd (which are relative to child position within the parent element) or can use expressions involving a variable n (such as 3n for every third child).
- li:first-child selects all li nodes that are the first child of their parent node.
- li:last-child likewise selects all li nodes that are the last child of their parent node.
- li:only-child selects all li nodes that are the only child of their parent node.

Selector	CSS	XPath
nth child nodes	ul:nth-child(2)	//ul/*[position() = 2]
first child nodes	li:first-child	//*/*[name() = "li" and position() = 1]
last child nodes	li:last-child	//*/*[name() = "li" and position() = last()]
only child nodes	li:only-child	//*/*[name() = "li" and count() = 1]

Form Filters

Form filters are a more convenient shorthand for other expressions.

- `:input` matches all input, textarea, select, and button elements.
- `:text`, `:hidden`, `:password`, `:radio`, `:checkbox`, `:submit`, `:image`, `:reset`, and `:file` all match input elements with their respective types.
- `:button` matches all button elements and input elements of type button.
- `:enabled` matches all form elements that are not disabled, `:disabled` matches those that are.
- `:checked` matches all checked radio and checkbox elements.
- `:selected` matches all selected option elements.

Selector	CSS	CSS Alt	XPath
all form elements	`:input`	`input, textarea, select, button`	`//input|//textarea|//select|//button`
form elements of specific types	`:text`	`input[type="text"]`	`//input[type="text"]`
button elements	`:button`	`button, input[type="button"]`	`//button|//input[type="button"]`
enabled elements	`:enabled`	`:not([disabled="disabled"])`	`//*[contains("input textarea select button", name()) and (not(@disabled) or @disabled!="disabled"])`
disabled elements	`:disabled`	`[disabled="disabled"]`	`//*[contains("input textarea select button", name()) and @disabled="disabled"]`
checked elements	`:checked`	`:input[checked="checked"]`	`//input[contains("checkbox radio", @type) and @checked="checked"]`
selected elements	`:selected`	`option[selected="selected"]`	`//option[@selected="selected"]`

Libraries

At this point, this chapter has covered CSS selectors to the extent that it explains all or a subset of those supported by a given library. This section reviews some available library implementations, where to find them, what feature set they support, and some advantages and disadvantages of using them.

Code examples in this section extract the href attribute values from the HTML sample in Listing 13.2.

Listing 13.2

```
1.  <div>
2.      <table>
3.          <tr>
4.              <td class="foo">
5.                  <div>
6.                      Lorem ipsum <span class="bar">
7.                      <a href="/foo/bar" id="one">One</a>
8.                      <a href="/foo/baz" id="two">Two</a>
9.                      <a href="/foo/bat" id="three">Three</a>
10.                     <a id="four">Four</a>
11.                 </span>
12.                 </div>
13.             </td>
14.         </tr>
15.     </table>
16. </div>
```

Zend\Dom\Query

One of the components of Zend Framework, the intent of this library is to provide a means for integration testing of applications based on the framework. It can also function independently and apart from the framework and provides the functionality needed in the analysis phase of web scraping.

The Zend\Dom\Query[3] component from the Zend Framework 2.x branch is at version 2.6.0 at the time of this writing and requires PHP 5.5 or higher. Zend_Dom_Query comes from the older Zend Framework 1.x branch, the last release of which was 1.12.20; it requires PHP 5.2.11 or higher. This section covers both versions.

This library makes extensive use of the _DOM extension_; see the related chapter of this book for more information. It supports XPath through use of the DOM extension's DOMXPath class and handles CSS expressions by transforming them into corresponding XPath expressions. It supports CSS 2, which excludes non-attribute filters.

It's also worth noting this library offers no retrieval functionality. All methods for introducing documents into it require that those documents be in string form beforehand. If you are already using Zend Framework, a readily available option for retrieval is the HTTP client library from Zend Framework, which is also discussed in this book.

Let's build an example using both versions of this library. We'll assume the variable $html contains the HTML sample shown earlier in this section.

---

[3]   Zend\Dom\Query: _https://docs.zendframework.com/zend-dom/query/_

In Zend Framework 2, you query for the href like this.

```
$dom = new \Zend\Dom\Query($html);
$results = $dom->execute('.foo .bar a[href]');
```

In Zend Framework 1, you query for the href like this.

```
$dom = new Zend_Dom_Query($html);
$results = $dom->query('.foo .bar a[href]');
```

We can iterate over $results in the same way using either version.

```
foreach ($results as $result) {
    // $result is a DOMElement instance representing the a element
    echo $result->getAttribute('href');
}
```

Zend\Dom\Query is available as a Composer package under the name zendframework/zend-dom.

No officially supported method exists to download the Zend_Dom package. The entire framework can be downloaded[4] and you can extract the directory for the Zend_Dom package from it. An unofficial Composer package is available under the name zf1/zend-dom.

Zend Framework components of both major versions are available under the New BSD License.

phpQuery

phpQuery[5] is heavily influenced by jQuery and maintains similarity to it insofar as its runtime environment being the server (as opposed to the client) allows. It requires PHP 5 (though it recommends 5.2) and the DOM extension as well as the Zend_Http_Client and Zend_Json components from Zend Framework, which you must install separately.

It supports a subset of CSS3 as well as most jQuery features, including plugin support. Other components include a CLI utility that makes functionality from the phpQuery library available from the command line and a server component for integrating with jQuery via calls made from it on the client side. Integration with Zend_Http_Client provides retrieval support.

Here is an example of using phpQuery to parse the earlier HTML example.

```
$doc = phpQuery::newDocument($html);
$results = $doc->filter('.foo .bar a[href]');

foreach ($results as $result) {
    // $result is a DOMElement instance representing the a element
    echo $result->getAttribute('href');
}
```

---

[4]   downloaded: _https://framework.zend.com/downloads/archives_
[5]   phpQuery: _http://code.google.com/p/phpquery/_

phpQuery was initially made available on Google Code and subsequently on GitHub before its development became inactive. Forks arose on GitHub to fix a variety of bugs. The most popular one is available as the Composer package electrolinux/phpquery[6] on Packagist. It's available under the MIT License.

PHP Simple HTML DOM Parser

The primary distinguishing trait of the PHP Simple HTML DOM Parser[7] is its requirements: PHP 5 and the PCRE extension (which is pretty standard in most PHP distributions). It has no external dependencies on or associations with other libraries or extensions, not even the standard XML extensions in PHP.

The implication of this is that PHP handles all parsing itself, so performance is not as good as libraries using a PHP extension. In environments where XML extensions (in particular the DOM extension) may not be available (which is rare), this library may be your sole option. It offers basic retrieval support using PHP's filesystem functions. If you wish to use these to access remote documents, you must enable the allow_url_fopen[8] PHP configuration setting.

Below is an example of using this library to parse the earlier HTML example.

```php
$doc = str_get_html($html);
$results = $doc->find('.foo .bar a[href]');

foreach ($results as $result) {
    // $result is an instance of the simple_html_dom_node class
    echo $result->href;
}
```

The documentation[9] for this library is good. You can also install it via an unofficial Composer package under the name sunra/php-simple-html-dom-parser[10]. It is available under the MIT License.

---

[6]   electrolinux/phpquery: *https://packagist.org/packages/electrolinux/phpquery*
[7]   *PHP Simple HTML DOM Parser:* *http://simplehtmldom.sourceforge.net*
[8]   allow_url_fopen: *http://php.net/allow_url_fopen*
[9]   *documentation:* *http://simplehtmldom.sourceforge.net/manual.htm*
[10]   sunra/php-simple-html-dom-parser: *https://phpa.me/sunra-simple-htmldom*

Chapter

14

Symfony Libraries

The Symfony project originated as a full-stack web framework in 2005. The last versions of the older 1.x and 2.x branches, 1.4.20 and 2.8.38, require PHP 5.2.4 and 5.3.9 respectively. The more recent 3.x and 4.x branches have 3.4.14 and 4.1.3 as their latest releases as of this writing, which require PHP 5.5.9 (or 7.0.8) and 7.1.3 respectively.

Symfony has evolved to offer a set of decoupled and reusable components on which that framework is now built. Some of these components can be useful in the context of web scraping.

CssSelector

XPath, detailed further in chapter 10, is a compelling way of querying markup documents for data. With that power comes verbosity and a somewhat steep learning curve. *CSS selectors*, detailed in chapter 13, are not as powerful as XPath but are generally easier to learn and more concise for everyday use cases.

The CssSelector[1] Symfony component programmatically converts CSS selector expressions to corresponding XPath expressions. While it does not support all valid CSS selectors, it supports enough of them to make it useful to developers who are familiar with CSS and prefer to avoid writing XPath expressions. You can use the XPath expressions generated by CssSelector with either of the *DOM* or *SimpleXML* extensions, detailed in chapters 10 and 11 respectively.

You can install CssSelector using Composer; the CssSelector documentation[2] includes instructions for doing so.

Listing 14.1 is an example of CssSelector in action.

Listing 14.1

```php
1. <?php
2. use Symfony\Component\CssSelector\CssSelectorConverter;
3.
4. $converter = new CssSelectorConverter;
5. $xpathExpression = $converter->toXPath('div.item > h4 > a');
6. $markup = '...';
7.
8. // DOM
9. $doc = new \DOMDocument;
10. $doc->loadHTML($markup);
11. $xpath = new \DOMXPath($doc);
12. $results = $xpath->query($xpathExpression);
13.
14. // SimpleXML
15. $xml = new \SimpleXMLElement($markup);
16. $results = $xml->xpath($xpathExpression);
```

- Instantiate the CssSelectorConverter class with no arguments.
- Pass a CSS selector expression contained within a string to the toXPath() method of the CssSelectorConverter instance.
- Receive a string containing an XPath expression corresponding to the supplied CSS selector expression that the toXPath() method returns.
- Use the returned XPath expression with either of the DOM or SimpleXML extensions as shown above.

This, on its own, is of limited use, but knowing how to use CssSelector is vital to use other Symfony components that build on it to offer more complex functionality.

For more information on the CssSelector component, see its documentation.

---

[1] CssSelector: *https://phpa.me/symfony-css-selector*
[2] CssSelector documentation: *https://phpa.me/symfony-css-selector-install*

DomCrawler

The Symfony DomCrawler component[3] makes it easier to navigate through and extract data from documents modeled by the _DOM_ (see chapter 10), such as XML and HTML documents. It natively supports filtering nodes using XPath expressions and, when you install the CssSelector component, CSS selectors as well.

As with CssSelector, you can install DomCrawler using Composer; the DomCrawler documentation[4] includes instructions for doing so.

Listing 14.2 is an example of basic usage of DomCrawler.

Listing 14.2

```php
1.  <?php
2.  use Symfony\Component\DomCrawler\Crawler;
3.
4.  $markup = '...';
5.
6.  $crawler = new Crawler($markup);
7.
8.  // $paragraphs will now reference a new Crawler instance with filtered nodes
9.  $paragraphs = $crawler->filterXPath('//body/p');
10.
11. // This is equivalent to the above call, but only works if you also have
12. // CssSelector installed
13. $paragraphs = $crawler->filter('body > p');
14.
15. // Crawler objects are iterable and yield DOMElement objects
16. foreach ($paragraphs as $paragraph) {
17.     echo $paragraph->textContent;
18. }
```

One significant value of DomCrawler is the supporting methods it provides on top of this functionality. Here are some noteworthy examples.

`Crawler->filter()` corresponds to `array_filter()`. It executes a callback against each node and returns a collection of nodes for which the callback returned `true`.

```php
$listItems = $crawler->filter('ul > li');

$evenListItems = $listItems->filter(
    function (Crawler $listItem, $index) {
        return $index % 2 == 0;
    }
);
```

---

[3]   DomCrawler component: _https://phpa.me/symfony-domcrawler_
[4]   DomCrawler documentation: _https://phpa.me/symfony-domcrawler-install_

Crawler->each() corresponds to array_map(). It executes a callback against each node and returns a collection of the callback's return values.

```
$listItemsText = $listItems->each(
   function (Crawler $listItem, $index) {
      return $listItem->text();
   }
);
```

Crawler->extract() extracts text and element attribute (e.g., class) values.

```
$textAndClasses = $listItems->extract(['_text', 'class']);
```

DomCrawler also provides special support for specific page elements which are useful in web scraping such as links, images, and forms.

Call Crawler->selectLink() with the link text or image alt attribute value. This method returns a new Crawler instance containing the link element.

```
// Locates a textual link using its text
$crawler = new Crawler('... <a href="...">Go here</a> ...');
$link = $crawler->selectLink('Go here')->link();
```

Call Crawler->link() on the result to get an instance of Symfony\Component\DomCrawler\Link for the link. This provides a getUri() method that returns the full URI of the page corresponding to the link's href attribute value.

```
// Locates an image link using its alt text
$crawler = new Crawler(
   '... <a href="..."><img src="..." alt="Also go here"></a> ...'
);
$link = $crawler->selectLink('Also go here')->link();
```

Images work in a similar manner, but use Crawler->selectImage() and Crawler->image() instead of Crawler->selectLink() and Crawler->link() respectively. The Symfony\Console\DomCrawler\Image class provides the same getUri() method as its Link counterpart.

```
// Locates an image using its alt text
$crawler = new Crawler(
   '... <img src="..." alt="This is an image" /> ...'
);
$link = $crawler->selectImage('This is an image')->image();
```

Forms are a bit more complex, but useful if you want to extract data from a form or use a form to send data.

As with links and images, filter the form element you want to access, then call the Crawler->form() method on it to get an instance of the Symfony\Component\DomCrawler\Form class.

We can locate the form submit button by its label with `$crawler->selectButton()`.

```
$crawler = new Crawler('... <input type="submit" value="Submit" /> ...');
$form = $crawler->selectButton('Submit')->form();
```

We can also find it by `id` attribute value.

```
$crawler = new Crawler('... <input id="submit-form" type="submit" /> ...');
$form = $crawler->selectButton('submit-form')->form();
```

Here's how to extract data from the form once you have it.

Get the form action attribute or, if the form method is GET, a URL including a query string with all the form's current data.

```
$uri = $form->getUri();
```

We can get the form method.

```
$method = $form->getMethod();
```

Here's how to get the values of all form fields in a flat, single-dimensional array.

```
$values = $form->getValues();
```

We can get the values of all form fields as PHP interprets them upon submission. The Form class interprets field names using square brackets as arrays.

```
$values = $form->getPhpValues();
```

Programmatic manipulation of form data is also supported. The importance of this feature should become more obvious in the next section.

We can set more than one field value at once. Form->setValues() takes an associative array of values to set keyed by field name.

```
$form->setValues([
    'field' => 'value',
    'another_field' => 'another_value',
    'array_field[foo]' => 'foo_value',
    'array_field[bar]' => 'bar_value',
]);
```

We can also change each field individually based on the field type. The Form class implements \ArrayAccess such that particular fields are accessible by field name using array notation on a Form instance, e.g., `$form['text_field']`. Each field type has a corresponding class under the Symfony\Component\DomCrawler\Field subnamespace and has supporting methods specific to its corresponding type for manipulating the field value.

```
$form['text_field']->setValue('value');

$form['checkbox_field']->tick();
$form['checkbox_field']->untick();

$form['select_field']->select('option_value');

$form['multiselect_field']->select(['option_value', 'another_option_value']);

$form['file_field']->upload('/path/to/file');
```

BrowserKit

BrowserKit[5] builds on DomCrawler to handle making HTTP requests and interacting with elements contained in responses.

By default, BrowserKit does not provide a specific HTTP backend implementation. Instead, it provides an abstract Client class with an abstract doRequest() method that returns a Response object; subclasses must extend this class and provide their implementation of this method.

The purpose of this architecture is to allow for more than one HTTP backend implementation. For example, Symfony functional tests use BrowserKit. The HTTP backend implementation they use bootstraps Symfony in the same PHP process used to run the tests. This negates the need to go through a separate HTTP server and an entire HTTP request-response workflow to conduct a test, thus avoiding a potential pain point for performance.

Goutte

Goutte[6] (rhymes with "boot") is a library that provides an HTTP backend for BrowserKit using Guzzle (see *chapter 6*).

Goutte is primarily used in Symfony versions older than 4.3. In 4.3 and later versions, you should use the HttpClient library, which the next section covers. Goutte version 3 works with PHP 5.5+ and Guzzle 6+, version 2 with PHP 5.4 and Guzzle 4-5, and version 1 with PHP 5.3 and Guzzle 3.

Like the other components in this chapter, you can install Goutte using Composer; see the Goutte installation instructions[7].

Let's look at some examples of what you can do with Goutte. First, you need to instantiate GoutteClient.

---

[5]   BrowserKit: *https://phpa.me/symfony-browserkit*
[6]   Goutte: *https://github.com/FriendsOfPHP/Goutte*
[7]   Goutte installation instructions: *https://phpa.me/goutte-install*

```
use Goutte\Client as GoutteClient;
use GuzzleHttp\Client as GuzzleClient;

$goutte = new GoutteClient;
```

Goutte can use a provided Guzzle client instance, e.g., if you want to use a custom configuration.

```
$guzzle = new GuzzleClient(['timeout' => 10]);
$goutte->setGuzzleClient($guzzle);
```

Goutte can then make requests with Guzzle and then follow links in responses.

```
$crawler = $goutte->request('GET', 'https://github.com');

$link = $crawler->selectLink('Sign in')->link();
$crawler = $goutte->click($link);
```

You can also submit forms in responses using BrowserKit.

```
$form = $crawler->selectButton('Sign in')->form();
$crawler = $client->submit($form, [
    'login' => 'username',
    'password' => 'redacted',
]);
```

Goutte has little documentation of its own and primarily references documentation for BrowserKit and DomCrawler. Beyond that, its source code is the closest thing to documentation that's available.

If you would rather provide your HTTP backend implementation instead of using Goutte, you can install BrowserKit directly using Composer[8].

HttpClient

HttpClient[9] is an HTTP client library that implements PSR-18[10]. As of Symfony 4.3, BrowserKit offers optional integration with HttpClient that negates the need for Goutte.

HttpClient is the actual HTTP client implementation.

```
use Symfony\Component\BrowserKit\HttpBrowser;
use Symfony\Component\HttpClient\HttpClient;

$client = HttpClient::create();
```

---

[8]   Composer: *https://symfony.com/components/BrowserKit*
[9]   HttpClient: *https://github.com/symfony/http-client*
[10]   PSR-18: *https://www.php-fig.org/psr/psr-18/*

HttpBrowser is an implementation of BrowserKit's AbstractBrowser class that integrates with HttpClient.

```
$browser = new HttpBrowser($client);
```

AbstractBrowser offers the same API as Goutte\Client for making requests and following links in responses.

```
$crawler = $browser->request('GET', 'https://example.com/');

$link = $crawler->selectLink('Sign in')->link();
$crawler = $browser->click($link);
```

Similarly, we can submit forms in responses using BrowserKit.

```
$form = $crawler->selectButton('Sign in')->form();
$crawler = $browser->submit($form, [
    'login' => 'username',
    'password' => 'redacted',
]);
```

At the time of this writing, HttpClient has no documentation of its own. Consult this presentation[11] or the HttpClient source code for more information on using it independently from BrowserKit.

Panther

BrowserKit simulates the HTTP traffic and some of the user interactions that can occur within a web browser without using an actual web browser. As a result, it often has better performance, but can be suboptimal for some use cases, such as scraping data from a website heavily powered by client-side code.

Panther, by contrast, is a Symfony library that interacts with an actual web browser by leveraging the FaceBook PHP WebDriver library. By default, Panther ships with a version of ChromeDriver, which facilitates interaction with a local Google Chrome installation. You can use it to power either a standard, visible Chrome instance, or a headless Chrome instance that runs in the background.

Panther implements the same APIs as BrowserKit and DomCrawler, so it feels familiar to users of those libraries; you can adapt most earlier examples in this chapter to use Panther with only minor changes to the client instantiation.

Panther does not support all the same operations[12] as BrowserKit and DomCrawler, and throws an exception if you call a method for an unsupported operation. That said, Panther does support

---

[11]   this presentation: https://phpa.me/symfony-httpclient-prez
[12]   operations: https://phpa.me/symfony-panther-limits

some features BrowserKit does not, such as taking screenshots and injecting JavaScript code into loaded pages at runtime.

To use Panther, install the Composer package symfony/panther.

$client is an instance of Symfony\Component\Panther\Client, which has the same API as Symfony\Component\BrowserKit\Client.

```
$client = \Symfony\Component\Panther\Client::createChromeClient();
```

$crawler is an instance of Symfony\Component\Panther\DomCrawler\Crawler which has the same API as Symfony\Component\DomCrawler\Crawler.

```
$crawler = $client->request('GET', 'https://api-platform.com');
```

For example, we can block execution while waiting for a page element matching this selector to load.

```
$client->waitFor('.support');
```

Panther can execute arbitrary JavaScript code and exchange data between it and PHP.

```
$hostname = $client->executeScript('return window.document.location.hostname;');
$client->executeScript('console.log(arguments);', [ 'foo', null, 42, true ]);
```

It can even take a screenshot of the loaded page and store it at the specified file path.

```
$client->takeScreenshot('screen.png');
```

While building your web scraping application from scratch and debugging existing ones are useful skills to have, it's also often useful to be able to build a functional application or proof-of-concept in a short amount of time. The Symfony component libraries discussed in this chapter provide a significant amount of functionality out of the box, can make for concise and readable source code, and are a great foundation on which to build your applications.

Chapter

15

PCRE Extension

Some markup documents may be so hideously malformed that they're not usable by an XML extension. Other times, you may want to check the data you've extracted to ensure it's what you expect. Changes to the structure of markup documents may be significant, to the point where your CSS or XPath queries return no results. They may also be small and subtle, such that while you do get query results, they contain less or different data than intended.

While you can handle either of these tasks with basic string handling functions and comparison operators, in most cases the implementation would prove to be messy and unreliable. **Regular expressions** provide a syntax[1] consisting of **meta-characters** whereby you can express patterns within strings flexibly and concisely. This chapter deals with regular expressions as they relate to the Perl-Compatible Regular Expression (PCRE) PHP extension in particular.

A common bad practice is to use regular expressions and nothing else to extract data from markup documents. While this may work for simple scripts intended for limited use, it's more difficult to maintain and less reliable in the long term. Regular expressions were not designed for this

---

[1]   syntax: *http://php.net/reference.pcre.pattern.syntax*

purpose, whereas other markup-specific extensions discussed in previous chapters are more suited for the task. It's a matter of using the best tool for the job, and to that end, you should avoid this practice.

> **POSIX Extended Regular Expressions**
>
> *PHP developers often cut their teeth on regular expressions using the POSIX regular expression extension, also called the ereg extension. PHP 5.3 deprecated functions from this extension and PHP 7 removed them altogether in favor of those in the PCRE extension, which are faster and provide a more powerful feature set. Aside from differences in syntax for some special character ranges, most ereg expressions work with preg functions if you add expression delimiters, which the next section covers.*

Pattern Basics

Let's start with something simple: detection of a substring anywhere within a string.

You can use strpos() for substring detection.

```
$present = (strpos($string, 'foo') !== false);
```

You can do the same with a PCRE function and a basic regular expression.

```
$present = (preg_match('/foo/', $string) == 1);
```

Notice the pattern in the preg_match() call is like the string used in the strpos() call. The former uses / on either side of the pattern to indicate its beginning and end. The first character in the pattern string is the **pattern delimiter** and can be any character you specify. When choosing what you want to use for this character (/ is the most common choice), bear in mind you will have to escape it (covered in the Escaping section later) if you use it within the pattern. This will make more sense a little later in the chapter.

A difference between the two functions used in this example is strpos() returns the location of the substring within the string beginning at 0 or false if the substring is not contained within the string. This requires the use of the === operator to tell whether the substring exists at the beginning of the string or does not exist in the string at all. By contrast, preg_match() returns the number of matches it finds. This will be either 0 or 1 since preg_match() stops searching once it finds a match.

Anchors

You may want to check for the presence of a pattern at the beginning or end of a string rather than checking to see if the string contains the pattern anywhere within it. The meta-characters for this are collectively referred to as **anchors**.

You can check for a match at the beginning of the string with a basic string function. Note the triple equals. If the string is not found, `strpos()` returns `false` but `false == 0` evaluates to `true`.

```
$start = (strpos($string, 'foo') === 0);
```

This is the same functionality with the ^ anchor in `preg_match()` and no type juggling gotchas. The presence of ^ (also called the circumflex or caret character) at the beginning of an expression within a pattern indicates that matching should start at the beginning of a string.

```
$start = (preg_match('/^foo/', $string) == 1);
```

In this example, we look for a match at the end of the string with basic string functions.

```
$end = (substr($string, - strlen('foo')) == 'foo');
```

Likewise, $ indicates that matching of an expression within a pattern should stop at the end of a string. Here is a regular expression looking for `foo` at the end of a string with the `preg_match()` function.

```
$end = (preg_match('/foo$/', $string) == 1);
```

When you use ^ and $ together, the entirety of `$string` must match the pattern.

```
$equal = (preg_match('/^foo$/', $string) == 1);
```

Start of String or Line

It's important to note the behavior of these two operators can vary. By default, they match the beginning and end of `$string`. If you use the multi-line modifier, they match the beginning and end of each line in `$string` instead. The Modifiers section of this chapter details this further.

Alternation

It's possible to check for more than one expression simultaneously in a single pattern, also called **alternation**, using the pipe meta-character |.

This regular expression matches `'foo'` or `'bar'` or `'baz'` anywhere in `$string`.

```
$matches = (preg_match('/foo|bar|baz/', $string) == 1);
```

^ and $ are not implicitly applied to all expressions in an alternation. The first block in the following example applies ^ to `'foo'` but not `'bar'`; because `'abar'` contains `'bar'`, it matches the latter half of the alternation and results in a return value of 1. The second block applies ^ to both 'foo' and 'bar'; since 'abar' begins with neither 'foo' nor 'bar', it returns 0.

```
// $result == 1
$result = preg_match('/^foo|bar/', 'abar');

// $result == 0
$result = preg_match('/^foo|^bar/', 'abar');
```

Repetition and Quantifiers

Part of a pattern may or may not be present, or may have consecutive instances. We call this **repetition** and it involves using meta-characters collectively referred to as **quantifiers**.

This regular expression matches 'a' zero times or one time if present.

```
$matches = (preg_match('/a?/', $string) == 1);
```

This matches a zero or more times.

```
$matches = (preg_match('/a*/', $string) == 1);
```

This preg_match() call matches a one or more times.

```
$matches = (preg_match('/a+/', $string) == 1);
```

This expression matches a zero times or one time if present, same as ?.

```
$matches = (preg_match('/a{0,1}/', $string) == 1);
```

This matches a zero or more times, same as *.

```
$matches = (preg_match('/a{0,}/', $string) == 1);
```

This expression matches a one or more times, same as +.

```
$matches = (preg_match('/a{1,}/', $string) == 1);
```

We can also match a exactly two times.

```
$matches = (preg_match('/a{2}/', $string) == 1);
```

Any use of curly brackets that is not of the form {X}, {X,}, or {X,Y} functions as a literal string within the pattern.

Subpatterns

You'll notice in the examples from the previous section that each uses a single character. This is because the chapter hasn't introduced **subpatterns** yes. To understand these, it's best to look at an example that doesn't use them in order to understand the effect they have on how the pattern matches.

The following regular expression matches 'a' follow by one or more instances of 'b'.

```
$matches = (preg_match('/ab+/', $string) == 1);
```

Without subpatterns, there would be no way to match, for example, one or more instances of the string 'ab'. Subpatterns solve this problem by allowing you to group individual parts of a pattern using parentheses.

With one expression, we can match the strings 'foo' or 'foobar'.

```
$matches = (preg_match('/foo(bar)?/', $string) == 1);
```

This matches ab or ac.

```
$matches = (preg_match('/a(b|c)/', $string) == 1);
```

This expression matches ab, ac, abb, abc, acb, acc, and more.

```
$matches = (preg_match('/a(b|c)+/', $string) == 1);
```

Matching

Subpatterns do a bit more than let you define parts of a pattern to which alternation or repetition apply. When you have a match, it's possible to get the substring from the original string that matched the entire pattern as well as substrings matching subpatterns.

```
if (preg_match('/foo(bar)?(baz)?/', $string, $match) == 1) {
    print_r($match);
}
```

The third parameter to preg_match(), $match, receives an array of match data. If a match occurs, that array contains at least one element: the entire substring which matched the pattern. Any elements that follow are subpattern matches with an index corresponding to that subpattern's position within the pattern. That is, the first subpattern will have the index 1, the second subpattern will have the index 2, and so on.

If a pattern is conditional (i.e., uses ?) and not present, it will either have an empty element value in the array or no array element at all.

In this first example, the (bar)? subpattern ends the entire pattern and is not matched. Thus, it has no entry in $match.

```
if (preg_match('/foo(bar)?/', 'foo', $match) == 1) {
    // $match == ['foo'];
}
```

In this second example, the (bar)? subpattern does not end the entire pattern and is not matched. Thus, it has an empty entry in $match.

```
if (preg_match('/foo(bar)?(baz)?/', 'foobaz', $match) == 1) {
    // $match == ['foo', '', 'baz'];
}
```

Subpatterns can also contain other subpatterns.

```
if (preg_match('/foo(ba(r|z))?/', 'foobar', $match) == 1) {
    // $match == ['foobar', 'bar', 'r'];
}
```

Aside from passing $match to print_r(), or a similar function, an easy way to tell what a subpattern's position will be in $match is to count the number of opening parentheses in the pattern from left to right until you reach the desired subpattern.

Using the syntax shown above, subpatterns are **captured** (i.e., have their own element in the array of matches). You can capture up to 99 subpatterns and use up to 200 subpatterns, captured or no, in an expression. While this realistically shouldn't become an issue, it's best to denote subpatterns that do not require capture using (?: instead of (to begin them.

You may also assign meaningful names to subpatterns which for captured subpatterns become their keys in the array of matches. To assign a name to a subpattern, begin it with the syntax (?P<name> instead of (where name is the name you want to assign to that subpattern. This makes code using matches more expressive and easier to maintain as a result.

Below is an example of parsing each segment of a U.S. phone number using named subpatterns.

```
$pattern = '/(?P<area>[0-9]{3})-(?P<office>[0-9]{3})-(?P<line>[0-9]{4})/';
if (preg_match($pattern, '123-456-7890', $match) === 1) {
    // $match = ['area' => '123', 'office' => '456', 'line' => '7890'];
}
```

Escaping

There may be instances where you want to include literal characters in patterns that are otherwise interpreted as meta-characters. You can do this via a \ meta-character.

Use one \ to match a literal [.

```
$matches = (preg_match('/\[/', $string) == 1);
```

Matching a literal \ is more complex. It's necessary to double-escape \ in the following example because PHP interprets the string \\ to be a single backslash whether used in a regular expression or not.

```
$matches = (preg_match('/\\\\/', $string) == 1);
```

In other cases, you don't need to escape \ for PHP to interpret the escape sequence properly. This matches expression delimiter /.

```
$matches = (preg_match('/\//', $string) == 1);
```

This matches any of the standard escape sequences \r, \n, or \t for carriage return, new line, or tab characters.

```
$matches = preg_match('/\r|\n|\t/', $string);
```

> **Double Escaping**
>
> *For more information on the reasoning behind the double-escape example in this section, see the PHP Language reference section about strings[2] and the Backslash section[3] about regular expressions.*

Escape Sequences

If you want to match a single character that could be any from a group of characters, there are three ways you can do it.

The first way involves using the . (period) meta-character, which will match any single character except a line feed ("\n") without the use of modifiers (which this chapter covers later). You can use quantifiers with this for repetition as you can with any other character.

The second way requires using special escape sequences that represent a range of characters. Aside from the escape sequences mentioned in the previous section's examples, here are some that are commonly used.

---

[2]   strings: https://phpa.me/string-types
[3]   Backslash section: http://php.net/regexp.reference

Sequence	Description
\d	A digit, 0 through 9.
\h	A horizontal whitespace character, such as a space or a tab.
\v	A vertical whitespace character, such as a carriage return or line feed.
\s	Any whitespace character, i.e. of all characters represented by \h and \v.
\w	Any letter or digit or an underscore.

Each of these escape sequences has a complement represented by the capital letter.

Sequence	Description
\D	A non-digit character.
\H	A non-horizontal whitespace character.
\V	A non-vertical whitespace character.
\S	A non-whitespace character.
\W	A character that is not a letter, digit, or underscore.

The third and final way involves using **character ranges**, which are characters within square brackets ([and]). A character range represents a single character, but like normal single characters, they can have repetition applied to them.

This example matches the same as \d, a single digit.

```
$matches = (preg_match('/[0-9]/', $string) == 1);
```

Similarly, this character range matches the same as \w.

```
$matches = (preg_match('/[a-zA-Z0-9_]/', $string) == 1);
```

Ranges are respective to ASCII (American Standard Code for Information Interchange). In other words, the ASCII value for the beginning character must precede the ASCII value for the ending character. Otherwise, PHP emits the warning "Warning: preg_match(): Compilation failed: range out of order in character class at offset n", where n is a character offset within the regular expression.

Within square brackets, single characters and special ranges exist side by side with no delimiter, as shown in the second example above. You can use the escape sequences mentioned earlier such as \w both inside and outside square brackets.

ASCII Ranges

This is an ASCII lookup table: http://www.asciitable.com.

The examples below illustrate two other noteworthy points about character ranges.

You can use a literal] in a character range like so:

```php
$matches = (preg_match('/[\]]/', $string) == 1);
```

To negate a character range, use ^ as the first character in that character range. (Yes, this can be confusing since ^ is also used to denote the beginning of a line or entire string when it's not used inside a character range.) Note that negation applies to all characters in the range. In other words, a negated character range means "any character that is not any of these characters." For example, using ^ in the range below matches any character that is not an a.

```php
$matches = (preg_match('/[^a]/', $string) == 1);
```

To use a literal ^ character in a character range, either escape it as you do other meta-characters or do not use it as the first or sole character in the range.

```php
$matches = (preg_match('/[\\^]/', $string) == 1);
$matches = (preg_match('/[a^]/', $string) == 1);
```

Ctype Extension

Some simple patterns have equivalent functions available in the Ctype library. These generally perform better and you should use them over PCRE when appropriate. See the Ctype documentation[4] for more information on it and the functions it offers.

Modifiers

The reason for having pattern delimiters to denote the start and end of a pattern is the pattern precedes **modifiers**[5] that affect the matching behavior of meta-characters. Here are a few modifiers that may prove useful in web scraping applications.

Modifier	Description
i	Any letters in the pattern match both uppercase and lowercase regardless of the case of the letter used in the pattern.
m	^ and $ match the beginning and ends of lines within the string (delimited by line feed characters) rather than the beginning and end of the entire string.
s (lowercase)	The . meta-character will match line feeds, which it does not by default.
S (uppercase)	Analyze the pattern in more depth to speed up later matches with that pattern. Useful for patterns used more than once.

---

[4] *ctype documentation: http://php.net/ctype*
[5] **modifiers**: *http://php.net/reference.pcre.pattern.modifiers*

Modifier	Description
U	By default, the quantifiers * and + behave in a manner referred to as "greedy." That is, they match more characters rather than fewer where possible. This modifier forces the latter behavior.
u	Assumes pattern strings are UTF-8 encoded strings.

The example below matches because of the i modifier, which means the pattern ignores case and matches 'a' and 'A'.

```
$matches = (preg_match('/a/i', 'A') == 1);
```

This chapter has covered the most essential aspects of regular expressions which apply to validation of scraped data. More advanced aspects of regular expressions may be useful in other areas. You should review the PCRE section of the PHP manual further. For an excellent book on regular expressions, see *Mastering Regular Expressions,* by Jeffrey E. F. Friedl—ISBN 0596528124.

Chapter

16

Practical Applications

Chapters preceding this one lay out information and examples about individual skills required to build a web scraping application. This chapter brings that information into context with more complete examples of a variety of applications.

Crawler

The origins of the common web scraping application known as a **crawler** date back to the first commercialization of the World Wide Web. Some of the first search engines had modest beginnings as organized collections of content that were manually curated by human beings. When the internet took off, its growth proved too explosive for humans to keep up with. At that point, we turned to machines to handle seeking out and analyzing new content for us to consume.

While specific implementations vary, the basic functionality of most crawlers is the same: retrieve the content for a given URL, analyze it, extract any URLs that are present, and repeat the process for each URL found. Crawlers are often used to populate databases used for search and supplemented with analyses to rank search results for relevance or recency.

With regard to architecture, a crawler typically consists of these components.

1. A data store, often a queue server, holds URLs to retrieve and content retrieved from URLs to analyze.

2. A mechanism seeds the data store with one or more URLs to retrieve, which instigates the crawling process.

3. A process removes URLs from the data store, retrieves their content, and places it in the data store for analysis.

4. A process removes content from the data store, extracts URLs from it, and adds them to the data store for retrieval.

5. A mechanism to track previously retrieved URLs to prevent potential repeated or circular retrieval operations.

Once the retrieval process begins, it and the analysis process feed each other: the analysis process gets the content it analyzes from the retrieval process, while the retrieval process gets further URLs to retrieve from the analysis process. When the analysis process is unable to find URLs not already retrieved, it ceases to feed the retrieval process, causing both to stop their respective activities.

Example

Let's look at an example of a naïve crawler.

First, let's use a command line script to seed the data store.

Listing 16.1

```php
1. <?php
2. // seed_crawler.php
3.
4. // Usage: php seed_crawler.php http://foo.com http://bar.com
5.
6. // This function adds a URL to whatever data store you choose to use.
7. // It may also handle ensuring that no duplicate URLs are added.
8. function put_url(string $url) {
9.     // ...
10. }
11.
12. // Remove the filename of this script from arguments passed to it
13. array_shift($argv);
14.
15. // Add the rest of the arguments, assumed to be URLs, to the data store
16. foreach ($argv as $url) {
17.     put_url($url);
18. }
```

Next, let's use a second command line script to handle retrieving content for URLs in the data store.

Listing 16.2

```php
1.  <?php
2.  // retrieve.php
3.
4.  // Usage: php retrieve.php
5.
6.  // This function removes a URL from the data store and returns it.
7.  // It may also handle ensuring that no duplicate URLs are returned.
8.  function get_url(): ?string {
9.      // ...
10. }
11.
12. // Adds content retrieved from a URL to the data store for analysis.
13. function put_content(string $content) {
14.     // ...
15. }
16.
17. // See chapter 6 for more on Guzzle
18. $client = new \GuzzleHttp\Client;
19.
20. while (true) {
21.     // Fetch a URL to retrieve
22.     $url = get_url();
23.
24.     // If the data store is out of URLs to retrieve, terminate
25.     if (!$url) {
26.         break;
27.     }
28.
29.     // Output the URL to make script activity visible
30.     echo $url, PHP_EOL;
31.
32.     // Fetch the URL
33.     $response = $client->get($url);
34.
35.     // There should be some verification of the response here, e.g., that the
36.     // status code is 200-level and the response body is non-empty
37.
38.     // Extract body content from the response
39.     $contents = $response->getBody()->getContents();
40.
41.     // Add the content to the data store for analysis
42.     put_content($content);
43. }
```

Let's use a third command line script to extract URLs from retrieved content and add them to the data store.

Listing 16.3

```php
1.  <?php
2.  // analyze.php
3.
4.  // Usage: php analyze.php
5.
6.  // Removes content for a single URL from the data store and returns it.
7.  function get_content(): ?string {
8.      // ...
9.  }
10.
11. // This is identical to the function of the same name from seed_crawler.php.
12. // Ideally, it should be defined in a central location and imported where needed.
13. function put_url(string $url) {
14.     // ...
15. }
16.
17. use Symfony\Component\DomCrawler\Crawler;
18.
19. while (true) {
20.     // Fetch content from the data store
21.     $content = get_content();
22.
23.     // If the data store has no more content to analyze, terminate
24.     if (!$content) {
25.         break;
26.     }
27.
28.     // See chapter 8 for more on DomCrawler
29.     $crawler = new Crawler($content);
30.
31.     // Filter all <a> elements and extract their href attribute values
32.     $urls = $crawler
33.         ->filterXPath('//a[@href]')
34.         ->each(function (Crawler $node) {
35.             // This may need to check for relative URLs and convert them to absolute URLs
36.             // See the URL sections of chapter 2 for more information
37.             return $node->attr('href');
38.         });
39.
40.     // For each extracted URL...
41.     foreach ($urls as $url) {
42.         // Output it to make script activity visible
43.         echo $url, PHP_EOL;
44.         // Queue it for retrieval
45.         put_url($url);
46.     }
47. }
```

Once `seed_crawler.php` runs to seed the queue, `retrieve.php` and `analyze.php` can run in parallel.

Scraper

While the term **scraper** is often used to refer to web scraping applications in general, you can also use it to refer to a specific type. Where a crawler is general in purpose and casts a wide net to find whatever data it can, a scraper is more specialized, generally targeted at a particular site or site format and designed to extract specific data.

Example

The website used for this example is odmp.org[1]. The site does not provide an API or archive of its data. It does provide a Terms of Use agreement[2] which allows for usage of its content without permission so long as the purposes fall under fair use.

> **robots.txt**
>
> *Some sites choose to follow an informal de-facto standard of including a* `robots.txt` *file. The purpose of this file is to communicate to crawlers which pages they should or should not index. It's "enforced" by the honor system, though there are some crawlers that ignore it. It's recommended your crawlers respect it as a courtesy to the people who maintain the site you are crawling.*
>
> *In some cases,* `robots.txt` *can also provide other useful information. On odmp.org, it provides the sole link on the site to an XML file that lists most pages on the site you would want to crawl. This list mitigates the need to extract URLs from retrieved pages when using a crawler, making it perform that much more efficiently and reliably.*
>
> *For more information on the robots.txt standard, visit http://www.robotstxt.org.*

The crawler for this example downloads data from the site and places it in a SQLite database to make it easy to search and query. You can download the source code by cloning the Git repository at *https://github.com/elazar/odmp-scraper*.

You can invoke the code from the command line, which is facilitated by its use of the Symfony Console component[3]. The entry point is in the file `src/DownloadCommand.php`, specifically the `execute()` method of the `DownloadCommand` class it contains.

Much of the code in `execute()` is rudimentary and uninteresting but necessary: checks on the file to receive extracted data, pagination calculations, etc. Let's look at the more interesting parts highlighted below.

---

[1]   *odmp.org: https://www.odmp.org*

[2]   *Terms of Use agreement: https://www.odmp.org/info/terms-of-use*

[3]   *Symfony Console component: https://phpa.me/sym-console-component*

```
protected function execute(InputInterface $input, OutputInterface $output)
{
  // ...

  $crawler = $this->getCrawler(['from' => $year, 'to' => $year, 'o' => $offset]);
  $ending = $this->getEndingOffset($crawler);
  $results = $this->getResultsPage($crawler, $ending);

  // ...
}
```

On the site, a form in the upper right-hand corner enables the user to perform a general search. If such a search returns no results, such as one for a distinctive first name, the site presents the user with another search form with more advanced options. Submitting this form with no criteria reveals a paginated list of all results, where the URL reveals all available search parameters.

DownloadCommand uses this information in its getCrawler() method, one of the methods invoked in the code sample shown above, to retrieve result pages. Let's take a closer look at it.

Listing 16.4

```
1.  <?php
2.  use Goutte\Client;
3.  // ...
4.
5.  protected function getCrawler(array $overrides = [])
6.  {
7.      $base_url = 'https://www.odmp.org/search';
8.      $defaults = [
9.          'name' => '',
10.         'agency' => '',
11.         'state' => '',
12.         'from' => '1791',
13.         'to' => date('Y'),
14.         'cause' => '',
15.         'filter' => 'all',
16.      ];
17.      $parameters = array_merge($defaults, $overrides);
18.      $url = $base_url . '?' . http_build_query($parameters);
19.      $client = new Client;
20.
21.      return $client->request('GET', $url);
22.  }
```

First, getCrawler() constructs the URL of a results page using a base URL, an array of default search parameters, and an array of search parameters specific to the retrieved results page.

Next, it instantiates the Goutte\Client *class* (see chapter 14), invokes its request() method to request the results page, and returns an instance of the Crawler class from the *Symfony DomCrawler* component (see chapter 14) which contains the markup from that page.

Once getCrawler() returns the Crawler instance, execute() invokes another internal method, getEndingOffset(), and passes it the Crawler instance.

Listing 16.6

```
1. protected function getEndingOffset(Crawler $crawler)
2. {
3.     $p = $crawler->filterXPath('//p[contains(text(), "Displaying officers")]');
4.
5.     if (!count($p)) {
6.         return null;
7.     }
8.
9.     $p_text = $p->text();
10.
11.     if (preg_match('/(?:of|through) ([0-9]+)/', $p_text, $match)) {
12.         return (int) $match[1];
13.     }
14.
15.     return null;
16. }
17. // ...
```

The purpose of this method is to extract the total number of results for the queried year, so the crawler knows when to stop fetching pages. A results page element resembling the following contains this information.

```
<p>Displaying officers 1 through 25 of 23380 for search terms: <strong>"1791"
through "2018"</strong></p>
```

To extract the total, getEndingOffset() uses a combination of *XPath expressions* (see chapter 10) and *PCRE expressions* (see chapter 15) to locate the containing element and then parse the total from the element's text content.

Once execute() has the total, it passes the crawler and the total (assigned to the variable $ending) to getResultsPage().

Listing 16.6

```
1.  protected function getResultsPage(Crawler $crawler, $ending)
2.  {
3.      if ($ending === null) {
4.          return strpos($crawler->html(), 'No Matches Found') === false
5.              ? $this->getSingleResultPage($crawler)
6.              : [];
7.      }
8.
9.      $table = $crawler->filterXPath('//div[@id="pagination"]/../div/table');
10.
11.     return $this->getMultipleResultsPage($table);
12. }
```

If a search returns a single result, the site presents the data for that result directly. If the search returns more than one result, the site returns a table of those results. getResultsPage() does a small amount of parsing and checking to see which is the case and routes to an appropriate method for that case.

Let's take a look at the getSingleResultsPage() method.

Listing 16.7

```
1.  <?php
2.  // ...
3.  protected function getSingleResultPage(Crawler $crawler)
4.  {
5.      $header = $crawler->filterXPath('//div[@id="memorial_featuredInfo_right"]');
6.      $url = $crawler->filterXPath('//meta[@property="og:url"]/@content')->text();
7.      $name = $header->filterXPath('//h4')->text() . ' '
8.          . $header->filterXPath('//h3')->text();
9.
10.     if (preg_match('/, ([^,]+)$/', $crawler->filterXPath('//title')->text(), $match)
11.         && isset($this->states[$match[1]])) {
12.         $state_name = $match[1];
13.     } else {
14.         $p = $crawler->filterXPath('//b[contains(text(), "Location:")]/..');
15.
16.         if (count($p)) {
17.             $state_name = str_replace('Location: ', '', $p->text());
18.         }
19.     }
20.
21.     $state = empty($state_name) ? null : $this->states[$state_name];
22.     $eow = preg_match('/End of Watch: ([^<]+)/', $header->html(), $match)
23.         ? (new \DateTime(trim($match[1])))->format('Y-m-d')
24.         : null;
25.
```

```
26.    $cause = str_replace(
27.        'Cause: ', '', $crawler->filterXPath('//b[contains(text(), "Cause:")]/..'
28.            )->text());
29.
30.    $result = [[
31.        ':url' => $url,
32.        ':name' => $name,
33.        ':state' => $state,
34.        ':eow' => $eow,
35.        ':cause' => $cause,
36.    ]];
37.
38.    return $result;
39. }
```

This method is one of two containing the bulk of the data extraction logic, the other being getMultipleResultsPage().

The element represented by the $header variable contains some pieces of relevant data, such as $name and $eow. As such, the example filters $header first and then uses it to constrain searches for the data it contains.

Once it filters elements containing each piece of data, it uses a combination of PCRE and other string manipulation functions to remove field labels, demarcate where it expects data to end, format dates, and other operations.

It then places the parsed data into an associative array structured for INSERT operations against the SQLite database. It encloses that associative array in an enumerated array before returning it; the reason for this is so the same logic can process arrays returned by either of getSingleResultsPage() and getMultipleResultsPage().

getMultipleResultsPage() operates a lot like getSingleResultsPage(). As such, this chapter leaves reviewing the former as an exercise for the reader.

Acceptance Tests

Web scraping isn't always used to extract data or to interact with third-party sites; sometimes, you can use it to write automated tests for web applications you write yourself. These are **acceptance tests**, which interact with your application as a whole. While some of the information in this section is specific to tests, other information applies to writing web scraping applications using the same software.

Codeception

An example of a framework used for writing this type of test is Codeception[4], which uses *Guzzle* (see chapter 6) and *Symfony BrowserKit* (see chapter 14). Here's an example of what a test written with

[4]   Codeception: https://codeception.com

Codeception looks like. Note it supports using *CSS selectors* (see chapter 13) and *XPath* (see chapter 10) expressions to interact with page elements.

Listing 16.8

```php
1. <?php
2. class SigninCest
3. {
4.     public function tryToTest(AcceptanceTester $I)
5.     {
6.         $I->wantTo('test my page');
7.         $I->amOnPage('/login');
8.         // Specify values for form fields using their names
9.         $I->fillField('email','miles@davis.com');
10.        $I->fillField('password','P@$$WORD');
11.        // Identify elements using CSS selectors
12.        $I->click('#submit');
13.        // Or XPath
14.        $I->click('//[@id=submit]');
15.        $I->see('Thank you, Miles');
16.    }
17. }
```

This section is a small sample of what Codeception offers. It can fill out other types of form fields, grab text from pages, manipulate cookies, and has other useful features.

In the context of acceptance tests, Codeception can function in one of two ways.

The first is analogous to a scraper[5] in that it analyzes markup from and interacts with web applications without using an actual web browser, where the second instead does use a web browser[6]. The first method performs faster than the second and doesn't require any external software, but is also less ideal for interacting with applications that have a lot of client-side logic.

Let's take a look at a basic implementation of an acceptance test using the second method.

ChromeDriver

Limiting tests to running in the Google Chrome browser minimizes the amount of set up and configuration necessary to get a test to run, so we'll take that approach for this example.

If you haven't already, install Google Chrome[7] on your local system and bootstrap Codeception[8] within your project directory. Don't worry about updating Codeception configuration files yet; we'll get to that in a moment.

---

[5]   analogous to a scraper: *https://phpa.me/codeception-php-browser*
[6]   does use a web browser: *https://phpa.me/codeception-web-driver*
[7]   install Google Chrome: *https://www.google.com/chrome/*
[8]   bootstrap Codeception: *https://phpa.me/codeception-bootstrap*

Next, you'll need to install ChromeDriver. If it isn't available from your preferred OS package management system, you can install it manually. To do so, select the correct version[9] for your particular environment, go to the Downloads page[10], and download and extract the archive for your chosen version and operating system.

To invoke ChromeDriver, run this command from your terminal.

```
chromedriver --url-base=/wd/hub --port=4444
```

If port 4444 is not available on your system, be sure to replace the value of the `--port` flag with an open port.

ChromeDriver needs to be running before your test suite runs.

Now, open the `tests/acceptance.suite.yml` file generated by Codeception and change it to look like this.

```
actor: AcceptanceTester
modules:
    enabled:
        - WebDriver:
            browser: chrome
            port: 4444
            url: https://www.google.com
        - \Helper\Acceptance
```

Note that the generated `PhpBrowser` string is now `WebDriver`. The value of the `url` attribute underneath is now `https://www.google.com`, and `browser` and `port` attributes now exist on the same level as `url`.

Take care to keep indentation whitespace consistent, or Codeception may throw errors when you attempt to run your test. If you must run ChromeDriver on a port other than the default of 4444, be sure to update the `port` attribute in this configuration file to reflect that. Some systems may require further updates to this file; consult related documentation[11] for more information.

After you've made the necessary configuration changes, you can generate your first acceptance test suite by running this command in your terminal from the root directory of your project.

```
php vendor/bin/codecept g:cest acceptance First
```

This command creates the file `tests/acceptance/FirstCest.php`. Open that file and change its contents as in Listing 16.9.

---

[9] the correct version: https://phpa.me/chrome-driver-version
[10] the Downloads page: https://phpa.me/chrome-driver-download
[11] related documentation: https://phpa.me/codeception-web-driver-config

Listing 16.9

```
1. <?php
2. class FirstCest
3. {
4.     public function tryToTest(AcceptanceTester $I)
5.     {
6.         $I->wantTo('write my first acceptance test');
7.         $I->amOnPage('/');
8.         $I->submitForm('#tsf', ['q' => 'codeception']);
9.         $I->see('https://codeception.com/');
10.    }
11. }
```

Now, run your test from your terminal by issuing this command from the root directory of your project.

```
php vendor/bin/codecept run acceptance
```

You should see a Chrome window appear which opens the Google website, enters the value "codeception" into the search form, submits the form, and retrieves the results page. In your terminal, output like the following should appear.

```
Codeception PHP Testing Framework v2.5.5
Powered by PHPUnit 7.5.8 by Sebastian Bergmann and contributors.
Running with seed:

Acceptance Tests (1) --------------------------------------------
✓ FirstCest: Write my first acceptance test (4.20s)
----------------------------------------------------------------

Time: 5.08 seconds, Memory: 10.00 MB

OK (1 test, 1 assertion)
```

The terminal output includes the filename of the test suite without its file extension, the value passed to the $I->wantTo() call to describe the individual test, and the result and runtime of that test.

Other Solutions

While ChromeDriver is the simplest solution to set up, it's not the only option available.

If you want to test on Firefox, you'll need GeckoDriver[12].

---

[12] GeckoDriver: https://github.com/mozilla/geckodriver

If you want a server that can manage launching browsers locally or remotely for you, take a look at Selenium[13].

See related Codeception documentation[14] for more information on available solutions.

Actions

You can perform a number of possible actions[15] during a test by invoking methods of the AcceptanceTester parameter $I received by the test method. Below are brief descriptions of some of the more commonly used methods.

The term **locator** in some of these descriptions denotes a _CSS selector_ (see chapter 13), _XPath expression_ (see chapter 10), or other string used to locate a DOM element; see related documentation[16] for more information on other types of locators that Codeception supports.

Locator	Description
amOnPage($path)	Navigates to a specified path under the URL specified by the url setting in tests/acceptance.suite.yml.
amOnUrl($url)	Navigates to a specified URL.
checkOption($locator)	Ticks a checkbox referenced by a locator; see also uncheckOption($locator).
click($locator)	Clicks a link or button referenced by a locator.
fillField($locator, $value)	Enters a value into a text field or textarea.
makeScreenshot($name)	Takes a screenshot of the current window and saves it to a file.
selectOption($locator, $value)	Selects an option in a select menu or radio button group; see also unselectOption($locator, $value)
submitForm($locator[, $data])	Submits a form on the page, optionally with a given set of key-value pairs.
wait($seconds)	Wait for a specified number of seconds.
waitForElement($locator, $timeout)	Waits up to a specified number of seconds for an element referenced by a locator to appear.

---

[13] Selenium: _https://docs.seleniumhq.org/download/_
[14] related Codeception documentation: _https://phpa.me/codeception-local-testing_
[15] number of possible actions: _https://phpa.me/codeception-web-driver-actions_
[16] related documentation: _https://phpa.me/codeception-accept-click_

Grabbers

Some actions extract data from page elements. Here are some commonly used ones.

Grabber	Description
grabAttributeFrom($locator, $attribute)	Returns the value of a specified attribute from an element referenced by a locator.
grabCookie($cookie, $params)	Returns the value or specific parameter values for a specified cookie.
grabTextFrom($locator)	Returns the text contents of an element referenced by a locator.
grabValueFrom($locator)	Returns the value of a form field referenced by a locator.

Assertions

While they're used more for testing purposes than not, some actions function as assertions against specific properties of the current page. Here are some commonly used ones; most have a complementary method beginning with dontSee.

Assertion	Description
see($locator, $context)	Checks that the current page contains a given string, optionally within the context of a specified locator.
seeCheckboxIsChecked($locator)	Checks that a checkbox referenced by a locator is checked.
seeElement($locator)	Checks that an element referenced by a locator is visible on the current page.
seeElementInDOM($locator)	Checks that an element referenced by a locator is present on the current page, whether it's visible or not.
seeInField($locator, $value)	Checks that a text field or textarea contains a specified value; see also seeInFormFields($locator, $data).
seeOptionIsSelected($locator, $value)	Checks that a specified value is selected for a select menu or radio button group referenced by a locator.

Appendix A

Legality of Web Scraping

The legality of web scraping is a rather complicated question, mainly due to copyright and intellectual property laws. Unfortunately, there is no easy and completely cut-and-dry answer, mainly because these laws can vary between countries. There are, however, a few common points for examination when reviewing a prospective web scraping target.

First, websites often have documents known as Terms of Service (TOS), Terms or Conditions of Use, or User Agreements (hereafter known as TOS documents for the sake of reference). These are generally located in an out-of-the-way location like a link in the site footer, or a Legal Documents or Help section. These types of documents are more prevalent on prominent and more well-known web sites. Below are segments of several such documents from websites that explicitly prohibit web scraping of their content. These may have been updated or changed but provide a representative sample of the legalese you will see.

- "Don't misuse our Services. For example, don't interfere with our Services or try to access them using a method other than the interface and the instructions that we provide."
  – Google Terms of Service, "Using our Services" section, as of 2018-04-21

- "You will not collect users' content or information, or otherwise access Facebook, using automated means (such as harvesting bots, robots, spiders, or scrapers) without our prior permission."
  – Facebook Statement of Rights and Responsibilities, Safety section, as of 2018-04-21

- "Amazon or its content providers grant you a limited... license to access and make personal and non-commercial use of the Amazon Services. This license does not include ... any use of data mining, robots, or similar data gathering and extraction tools."
  – Amazon Conditions of Use, LICENSE AND ACCESS section as of 2018-04-21

- "You agree not to copy/collect CL content via robots, spiders, scripts, scrapers, crawlers, or any automated or manual equivalent (e.g., by hand)."
  – craigslist Terms of Use, USE section, as of 2018-04-21

- "In connection with using or accessing the Services you will not: ... use any robot, spider, scraper, data mining tools, data gathering and extraction tools, or other automated means to access our Services for any purpose, except with the prior express permission of eBay ..."
  – eBay User Agreement, "Using eBay" section, as of 2018-04-21

- "... you agree not to: ... access, monitor or copy any content or information of this Website using any robot, spider, scraper or other automated means or any manual process for any purpose without our express written permission ..."
  – Expedia, Inc. Web Site Terms, Conditions, and Notices, PROHIBITED ACTIVITIES section as of 2018-04-21

- "The foregoing licenses do not include any rights to: ... use any robot, spider, data miner, scraper or other automated means to access the Barnes & Noble.com Site or its systems, the Content or any portion or derivative thereof for any purpose ..."
  – Barnes & Noble Terms of Use, Section I LICENSES AND RESTRICTIONS as of 2018-04-21

Determining whether or not the website in question has a Terms of Service (TOS) document is the first step. If you find one, look for clauses using language similar to that of the above examples. Also, look for any broad "blanket" clauses of prohibited activities under which web scraping may fall, such as "data extraction" or "misuse."

If you find a TOS document and it does not expressly forbid web scraping, the next step is to contact representatives who have authority to speak on behalf of the organization that owns the website. Some organizations may allow web scraping assuming you secure permission with appropriate authorities beforehand. When obtaining this permission, it is best to obtain a document in writing and on official letterhead that clearly indicates it originated from the organization in question. This document has the most likely chance of mitigating any legal issues which may arise.

If intellectual property-related allegations are brought against an individual as a result of usage of an automated agent or information acquired by one, assuming the individual did not violate any TOS agreement imposed by its owner or related computer use laws, a court decision will likely boil down to whether or not the usage of said information is interpreted as "fair use" with respect to copyright laws in the geographical area in which the alleged offense took place.

Please note that these statements are very general and are not intended to replace the consultation of an attorney. If TOS agreements or lack thereof and communications with the website owner prove inconclusive, it is highly advisable to seek legal counsel prior to any attempts being made to launch an automated agent on a website. This risk is another reason why web scraping is a less-than-ideal approach to solving the problem of data acquisition and why it should be considered only in the absence of alternatives.

Some sites use license agreements to grant open or mildly restricted usage rights for their content. Well-known licenses to this end include the GNU Free Documentation license and the Creative Commons licenses. In instances where the particular data source being used to acquire data is not relevant, sources that use licenses like these should be preferred over those that do not, as legalities are significantly less likely to become an issue.

The second point of inspection is the legitimacy of the web site as the originating source of the data to be harvested. Even large companies with substantial legal resources, such as Google, have run into issues when their automated agents acquired content from sites illegally syndicating other sites. In some cases, sites attribute their sources, but in many cases, they do not.

For textual content, entering direct quotations that are likely to be unique from the site into major search engines is one method that can help to determine if the site in question originated the data. It may also provide some indication as to whether or not syndicating that data is legal.

For non-textual data, make educated guesses as to keywords that correspond to the subject and try using a search engine specific to that particular data format. Searches like this are not intended to be extensive or definitive indications, but merely a quick way of ruling out obvious syndication of an original data source.

Index

A

Acceptance Tests, 159–63, 167

Apache, 6, 12

ASCII, 148

authentication, 4, 6, 12, 16–19, 26, 35, 37, 52, 63, 80

  basic, 17

  credentials, 26, 35–37

  digest, 17, 19, 26

  identity, 13

  methods, 35

B

BrowserKit, 136–39

C

cache, 39, 50, 86

  content, 15, 37, 53

  internal DNS, 39, 45

Certificate Authority, 35, 63

  bundle, 63–64

  current bundle, 36, 64

chromedriver, 138, 160–62

Codeception, 159–63

Composer, 36, 64, 136–37

content encoding, 50, 85–86

Content-Type, 10, 12, 23–24, 50, 57, 59–60, 71–72

cookies, 4, 13, 34–35, 49, 51–52, 61–62, 73–74, 76–80, 160

  COOKIEFILE, 34–35

  data, 34–35, 51, 61, 76–77

  header, 13

  jar, 61

  name, 52, 61, 76

  objects, 77

  store, 51

  values, 35, 52

CSS, 122–26, 132, 141

  CSS2, 121

  CSS3, 121

  selectors, 4, 121–22, 124, 131, 133, 160, 163

Ctype Extension, 149

cURL, 27–44, 50, 52–53, 61, 63, 71, 80

  authentication, 35

  CURLOPT, 28–30, 33–41, 50

  DNS caching, 39

  Extension, 27–30, 32, 34–36, 38–40, 42, 44–46, 49, 51, 55, 75, 89

  PHP extension, 19, 27–28, 31, 35

  return value of, 33, 36

  session, 28–29

  set credentials, 35

  target server, 40

D

DateTime, 38, 158

deflate, 85

  encoding scheme, 86

DEFLATE algorithm, 86

denial-of-service attack, 86

php[architect] Books

The php[architect] series of books cover topics relevant to modern PHP programming. We offer our books in both print and digital formats. Print copy price includes free shipping to the US. Books sold digitally are available to you DRM-free in PDF, ePub, or Mobi formats for viewing on any device that supports these.

To view the complete selection of books and order a copy of your own, please visit: *http://phparch.com/books/*.

- **Security Principles for PHP Applications**
  By Eric Mann
  ISBN: 978-1940111612

- **Docker for Developers, 2nd Edition**
  By Chris Tankersley
  ISBN: 978-1940111568 (Print edition)

- **What's Next? Professional Development Advice**
  Edited by Oscar Merida
  ISBN: 978-1940111513

- **Functional Programing in PHP, 2nd Edition**
  By: Simon Holywell
  ISBN: 978-1940111469

- **Web Security 2016**
  Edited by Oscar Merida
  ISBN: 978-1940111414

- **Building Exceptional Sites with WordPress & Thesis**
  By Peter MacIntyre
  ISBN: 978-1940111315

- **Integrating Web Services with OAuth and PHP**
  By Matthew Frost
  ISBN: 978-1940111261

- **Zend Framework 1 to 2 Migration Guide**
  By Bart McLeod
  ISBN: 978-1940111216

- **XML Parsing with PHP**
  By John M. Stokes
  ISBN: 978-1940111162

- **Zend PHP 5 Certification Study Guide, Third Edition**
  By Davey Shafik with Ben Ramsey
  ISBN: 978-1940111100

- **Mastering the SPL Library**
  By Joshua Thijssen
  ISBN: 978-1940111001

www.ingramcontent.com/pod-product-compliance
Lightning Source LLC
LaVergne TN
LVHW062317060326
832902LV00013B/2268